BOSTON RED SOX

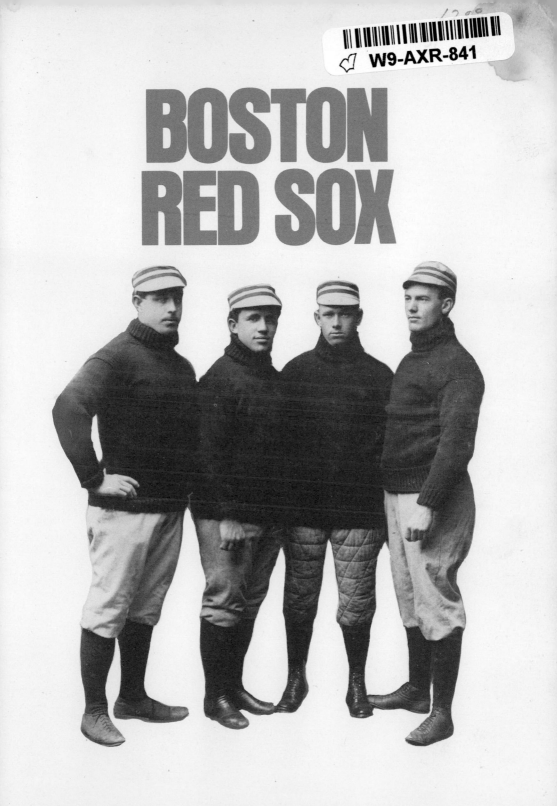

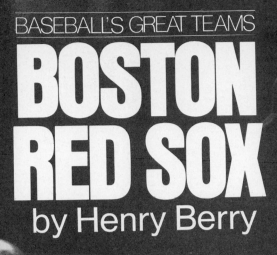

BASEBALL'S GREAT TEAMS

BOSTON
RED SOX

by Henry Berry

A Rutledge Book

Collier Books

A Division of Macmillan Publishing Co., Inc.
New York

Collier Macmillan Publishers
London

Library of Congress Cataloging in Publication Data
Berry, Henry.
   Boston Red Sox.
   1. Boston.   Baseball Club (American League)   I. Title.
GV875.B62B47   1975   796.357'64'0974461   74-34354
ISBN 0-02-029370-4

Macmillan Publishing Co., Inc.
866 Third Avenue, New York, N.Y. 10022
Collier-Macmillan Canada Ltd.
Boston Red Sox
is also published in a hardcover edition by
Macmillan Publishing Co., Inc.
First Collier Books Edition 1975
Printed in the United States of America

To my father, Harold J. Berry, who could always
find the time during the depth of the Depression
to take my brother and myself to Elizabeth Park
in Hartford and hit us fly balls.

Contents

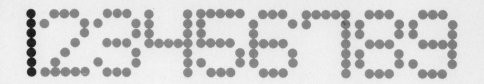

PLAY BALL

The Boston Red Sox were so named because they wore red baseball stockings and because they played their games at Jersey and Lansdowne Streets in the capital of Massachusetts. Today they still wear red stockings and still play in Boston, but they should be renamed. They should be the New England Red Sox.

If you had eavesdropped in the White Mountains or in the Berkshires or on Cape Cod that splendid early fall of 1967, you'd know. "Did yuh hear about Yaz last night?" and "My God, I think they may have killed Tony C!" From car radios in Brunswick, Maine, to transistors on the beaches of Nauset, Ken Coleman's broad "A's" were better known than the Kennedys'. The New Bedford *Standard Times* was one of many New England papers that plastered its sports pages with news of the unbelievable drive.

Oh, once the Red Sox had a rival for New England's baseball heart. Those were the turn-of-the-century days when Ban Johnson was just launching his American League and names like "Ole Hoss" Radbourne, "the Heavenly Twins," and "Orator" O'Rourke were household words. During the Patriots' Day (April 19) doubleheaders of 1904, three years after Johnson named his league, the American League entry in Boston (then called the Pilgrims or Puritans) drew 36,034 into its Huntington Avenue park while the Boston National League team (then called the Beaneaters) drew 5,667. With a few exceptions, New England has been American League country ever since. The final triumph came in 1948,

when the National League Boston Braves won the pennant and were decisively outdrawn by the Red Sox —who didn't. Exit the National League from the Hub.

The first two decades of Red Sox history had been ones in which the club had won more World Series (five) than any other team in baseball had.

Do you remember the Snodgrass Muff, Rough Carrigan, Carl Mays, the Golden Outfield, and a moon-faced kid from the streets of Baltimore who would end up better known than the President?

Then a blanket of gloom descended on New England as wheeler-dealer Harry Frazee started a shuttle between Boston and New York that turned the Yankees into the mightiest team in baseball, to the delight of the Yankees' baron, brewmaster "Uncle Jake" Ruppert.

"And who will you sell me today, Frazz?"

A young Yale graduate, Tom Yawkey, rescued the near bankrupt Sox with a bankroll that rivaled that of Ruppert. Lefty Grove, Jimmie Foxx, Joe Cronin, Heinie Manush, Rube Walberg, and Max Bishop were some of the greats whom Yawkey imported, and they livened up Fenway but rarely produced a contender and never a winner. Not until 1946 was there a pennant. Then a home-grown group of stars—Williams,

7

Pesky, Doerr, Hughson, and Ferriss —confidently overwhelmed the Yankees as if it was nothing unusual for a Boston team to humble the New Yorkers, only to be humbled themselves in the World Series by the underdog Cardinals.

Pesky stopped and Slaughter didn't—and Ted stopped hitting. That's all.

In 1948 and 1949, hopes for a pennant feast were dashed on the final day of the season. And then the Red Sox went hungry until 1967. Now, they have started to make respectability, if not ultimate triumph, a habit. The team of 1972 came ever so close before being doomed by its year-long problem—not being able to win in Tiger Stadium. In 1974, a September swoon denied a team that in August seemed on the verge of running away with the division flag. The Red Sox haven't won a World Series since the Twenty-sixth (Yankee) Division was in France in 1918, but they are flourishing again. The old park is loaded with supporters of El Tiant, Yaz, Rico, Lee, and a flock of kids who intend to become the new idols. These kids will be New Englanders, for New England owns the Red Sox. And should the kids make another run at a pennant, they will own New England.

123456789

BEGINNINGS

The New League's Plymouth Rock

As the man who formed the American League of Baseball Teams in 1900, hardheaded, hard-drinking, Machiavellian Bancroft Johnson was the somewhat reluctant parent of the Boston Red Sox (née Pilgrims).

Ban's original plans to expand and upgrade his Western League into a major circuit did not originally include a franchise in Boston. But

he soon heard that in an attempt to abort his new venture the National League was trying to resurrect the old American Association and place a team in the Hub. In the American Association the National League moguls hoped to have a second league that was strong enough to ruin Johnson's operation yet weak enough to be manipulated. (Doing business with the intemperate Johnson did not sit well with these autocrats.)

But in challenging Johnson they had challenged the wrong man. He immediately retaliated by moving his own proposed Buffalo franchise to New England.

To bankroll the new franchise Johnson prevailed upon a Mr. Arthur Somers, a coal, lumber, and shipping magnate, who was something of a Mr. Moneybags to the American League. Somers was the gentleman who had financed the new Cleveland franchise (in which Johnson is alleged to have invested rather heavily), as well as the Philadelphia entry of one Cornelius McGillicuddy, better known as Connie Mack. (John McGraw, at the time manager of the Baltimore Orioles and later of the National League New York Giants, criticized this last investment as ill-advised, but he would reassess that judgment in 1911 and 1913.) Somers had also advanced $10,000 to Charles Comiskey in Chicago. Indeed, the first six pennants in American League history were won by teams that owed their birth to Somers.

Obtaining a ball park for the fledgling Boston franchise was also an American League family affair. Hugh Duffy, who would manage the American League entry in Milwaukee, and former teammate Tom McCarthy (the two had been the "Heavenly Twins" of the Boston Beaneaters in the National League) located an area on Huntington Avenue owned by the New Haven Railroad. It was situated directly across from the park where Bill Cody would bring his Wild West Show, and therefore would prompt the great Red Sox fan-to-be, "Nuff Ced" McGreevey, to exclaim, "Who's going to play second base, Sitting Bull?" The lessee of the property turned out to be the same Cornelius McGillicuddy who managed the Athletics. And so, with

10

Above left: Connie Mack, right, Red Sox' early patron, meets rival John McGraw. *Opposite top:* American League mastermind, Ban Johnson. *Opposite bottom:* Fred Mitchell (born Fred Yapp).

more than a little help from its friends and/or competitors (businessmen of the era had not yet become wary of conflicts of interest), Boston had a franchise and a place to play. The only thing missing was a team.

You started a team in 1900 as you do today—by waving greenbacks at the stars in the other league. The Pilgrims (sometimes called the Puritans) fired an impressive opening salvo in the bidding war when they landed James Collins, the third baseman of the Beaneaters, as player-manager. They offered Jimmy $4,000 a year, a huge sum in 1900 and too much to resist for a man who solemnly stated, "I have myself and my family to think of first." Collins demanded and received in his contract a provision that stipulated he would receive the money as manager even if legal problems prohibited him from playing.

Then came the coup of coups. Frank Robison, custodian of both the Cleveland Spiders and the St. Louis Nationals, transferred his famous battery of Cy ("Farmer") Young and Lou Criger from Cleveland to St. Louis. The immortal Cy was very unhappy about having to move south ("Too damn hot," he said), and the Pilgrims quickly produced another $4,000 contract offer. Criger wanted to go where Cy went, and Boston ended up with the pair.

To complement the star pitcher, the Pilgrims went after the young pitching ace of the crosstown Beaneaters, "Big Bill" Dineen. Bill was a little apprehensive initially. Many years later he explained why he decided to wait awhile before jumping leagues: "Cy was considered the best in the game. If the new league folded, he still would have been all right, but I might have been in trouble." Dineen did jump the next year, and the Pilgrims gained the second of the two pitchers who would lead them to the pennant in 1903 (see pages 42-48) and 1904 (see pages 98-100).

They picked up shortstop Fred Parent from the Eastern League (the last survivor of the 1903 World Series, Freddy died in 1972) and second baseman Hobe Ferris in a clandestine move against the Cincinnati Reds. For the Pilgrims' first seven years, these two would excel as Boston's keystone combination.

From the Beaneaters came hard-hitting outfielders Chick Stahl and Buck Freeman. "The triumvirate [the group that owned the Beaneaters] don't like to pay their players much money," Stahl said pointedly. Another outfielder, Tommy Dowd, was lured from Cleveland, but he played only one season with the Pilgrims and contributed nothing more notable to Boston baseball than the memory of his nickname, "Buttermilk Tommy."

On April 26, 1901, at Baltimore, the Pilgrims played their first game. "Iron Man" Joe McGinnity and "Turkey Mike" Donlin of the Orioles (the team would move to New York and become the Highlanders in 1903) spoiled Boston's debut, 10-6. Cy Young and Freddy Mitchell pitched that first game for Boston. Never too successful as a pitcher, Mitchell was later the Cubs' manager against the Red Sox in the World Series of 1918. (His real name was Fred Yapp, but he abandoned it because "yapp" at the time was a slang expression for "jerk.")

May 8 was opening day for both the Pilgrims and the American League in Boston. The new team was greeted by the first of what has become a Red Sox tradition, a standing room audience. The Pilgrims opened with Young, and the Farmer held the visiting Athletics in check while the Pilgrims rattled out 19 hits. Young and company crushed landlord Connie Mack's charges 12-4. The Pilgrims had landed.

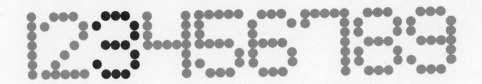

MILESTONES

The Rape of the Red Sox

For Sale

Every melodrama (and the Red Sox' story certainly qualifies as one) has its villain. To the fans of Boston, he is Harry Frazee, as infamous a character in New England as Benedict Arnold, Lizzie Borden, and Judge Sewall (the one who condemned the Salem witches). The great sportswriter Fred Lieb called Frazee the "evil genie." Less imaginitive observers might simply have typed him an outside agitator, for he was not a New Englander but a native of Peoria, Illinois.

Frazee was a baseball fan, but his first and all-consuming love was the theater. Unfortunately, Frazee's stage productions never had the promise or the success of his Red Sox. So, to finance his theatrical fiascos, Frazee sent player after player to New York and eventually gave Yankees owner and beer magnate Jake Ruppert the baseball dynasty that Boston might have had.

When Frazee bought the Red Sox from Joe Lannin after their World Series triumph of 1916, the team was in the midst of its most successful era—four world championships in seven years, 1912-18. Led by fireballing Joe Wood and their Golden Outfield of Duffy Lewis, Tris Speaker, and Harry Hooper, the Red Sox had won the pennant and World Series in 1912, then repeated in 1915 with a pitching staff that included a young dynamo from Baltimore, George Herman ("Babe")

Ruth. If it were not for the transfer of ownership, the team's future would have seemed as bright as its recent past, but Frazee brought some bad omens with him to Boston. The first was his previous venture into sports. He had been one of the sponsors of the heavyweight championship fight between Jack Johnson and Jess Willard in Havana the year before—a bout that, if not demonstrably fixed, left a moral stench comparable to the more immediate odor that sometimes rises from Back Bay at low tide. The second bad omen was the location of the Frazee Theater. It was not only in New York, where Harry spent most of his time, but on Forty-second Street, only two doors from the

Above: the evil genie and his friends. Left to right: Jake Ruppert, Commissioner Kenesaw ("Mountain") Landis, Cap Huston, and Frazee. *Right:* Red Sox manager Jack Barry, seen here as Holy Cross coach.

14

office of the New York Yankees—the hen house next to the fox den. Finally, Red Sox fans should have shifted uncomfortably when Frazee brought the treasurer of the Cort Theater in Chicago (in which Harry owned a substantial interest) to become the Red Sox' secretary. It was a clear indication that Frazee's sports and theater operations were interdependent. Another harbinger was the advertisements he plastered around Fenway Park for his shows. After the announcement of yet another player shipment to New York, a crusty Red Sox fan noted the sign for one unfortunate Frazee production, *My Lady Friends,* and commented, "Well they're the only friends the SOB has."

In the beginning at least, Frazee was more popular. Shortly after he bought the team, it became obvious that manager William ("Rough") Carrigan was indeed going back to Maine as he had threatened and that the Red Sox would need a replacement. Harry signed Jack Barry, who, like Carrigan, was a Holy Cross man and a very popular baseball figure in Boston. So far, so good. Then the rumor swept Boston that the Red Sox had offered Senators owner Clark Griffith $60,000 for the premier right hander, Walter Johnson. Commenting on the rumor (which he himself might have started), Frazee intoned, "Nothing is too good for the Boston fans," and those who didn't know better may have felt assured.

The Sox won a world championship in 1918, but New England was preoccupied with the ferocious fighting in France that summer and had little time for baseball. By the time the season ended, on Labor Day, the Twenty-sixth (Yankee) Divi-

sion had become the first National Guard unit to arrive in Europe, and news of the Argonne Forest overshadowed the exploits of Harry's world champs.

All but Frazee's note holders seemed to have forgotten the Sox. (Harry hadn't even paid Lannin for the ball club yet.) The importuning bill collectors started Frazee on his quest for funds, and the tantrum of a temperamental pitcher led him to Ruppert's hockshop with the Red Sox.

Carl Mays had been a 20-game winner for the Sox in both 1917 and 1918. He was also one of the heaviest-hitting pitchers in the league. But Carl was a brooder prone to paranoia, and when he pitched badly at the start of the 1919 season (by midseason he was 5-11), he somehow hatched the idea that the team was letting him down deliberately. On July 13, he jumped the team with a parting, "Tell [Ed] Barrow [Barry's successor as manager] I've gone fishing." The next day he was more direct. "I'll never pitch another game for the Red Sox," he said. And he was right.

Frazee was now in a quandary: what to do about his star pitcher who had just become worthless? He found the answer two doors down the block on Forty-second Street, at Yankee headquarters. For Mays, Jake Ruppert, and Cap Huston offered Frazee $40,000 and a couple of pitchers whose names are lost in the sands of time and mediocrity. The man who would never pitch again for the Red Sox was soon pitching (and how!) for the Yankees. Two years later, New York won the first of its many pennants, helped substantially by Mays's league-leading 27 victories.

The loss of Mays was indeed a blunder, but it seemed a mere over-

sight compared to Frazee's next deal—the sale of the greatest baseball player of all time, Babe Ruth. Some years later, Barrow told writer Tom Meany what happened. "I was at my home in Manhattan on a Sunday morning in January 1920 when I received a phone call from Frazee to meet him at the Hotel Knickerbocker at six in the evening."

16

Four that got away or, rather, were sent packing. *Clockwise from below:* shortstop Everett Scott, catcher Wally Schang, and pitchers Carl Mays and Waite Hoyt.

When Ed arrived, he found that Harry had been drinking rather heavily. "Simon [Frazee's name for Barrow], you're going to be sore as hell at me for what I'm going to tell you," Harry said.

Ed replied, "I've felt this in my bones for a long time, particularly since you called me at home this morning. You're going to sell the big fellow. I expected it, Harry, but let me tell you this: you're going to ruin yourself and the Red Sox in Boston for a long time to come."

"I can't help it; I'm up against the wall," Frazee replied. "I need money desperately. Ruppert and Huston are going to give me a hundred thousand dollars for Ruth, and besides that, Jake is going to give me a personal loan [in the form of a demand note] of three hundred and fifty thousand dollars."

A year later a resigned Ed Barrow joined the migration to New York himself, becoming the Yankees' general manager.

Until they sold Ruth, the Red Sox had won more World Series than any other team. Such a strong club might have survived the monumental loss of Ruth, but Frazee had only begun to peddle his players to Ruppert. Ruth hit an earth-shaking 54 home runs in 1920, but the Cleveland Indians won the pennant, so Ruppert solicited Frazee for more players. This time the Boston owner sent the Yankees hard-hitting catcher Wally Schang, future Hall of Famer Waite Hoyt, and utility infielder Mike McNally, a lesser light, whose most notable accomplishment in Boston had been pinch hitting for Ruth. In addition to cash Boston received an outstanding catcher, Muddy Ruel, but soon shuffled him off to Washington, where he became

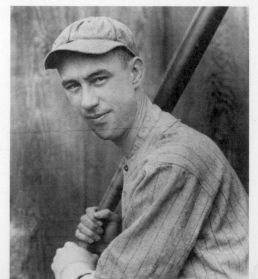

one of the American League's star receivers.

After Hoyt and Schang helped win a pennant for Ruppert in 1921 but failed to beat John McGraw's Giants in the World Series (despite Hoyt's 0.00 ERA in 27 innings), Frazee sent three more stars on the shuttle to New York: shortstop Everett Scott and pitchers "Bullet Joe" Bush and "Sad Sam" Jones. Scott would sparkplug the pennant-winning Yankees of 1922 and 1923; Bush would win 26 games in 1922 and Jones 21 in 1923. Once again, in addition to cash, the Red Sox received a valuable player—Roger Peckinpaugh—in return, and once again the player departed without having a chance to salvage the rapidly fading hopes of the Beantowners. Peckinpaugh belonged to Boston for one day, then was sent to Washington for Joe Dugan. In 1925, Peckinpaugh, on the pennant-winning Senators, was voted most valuable player in the league.

By that time Dugan too had proven too valuable for Frazee to keep. He moved to New York in July 1922 to assist the Yankees in their pennant fight with the St. Louis Browns, who were led by "Gorgeous George" Sisler. This was the best Browns team in history, but they couldn't match the Yanks' connections. When the Yanks needed help at third base, where 36-year-old Frank Baker had slipped drastically, Frazee dispatched Dugan in return for a bundle of cash to cover another theatrical misadventure. The Browns squawked, but Ruppert just smiled in his suds. The New Yorkers won the pennant, beating the runner-up Browns in 14 of 22 games. (Strangely, the mighty Yanks lost as many to the lowly Sox that year.)

But New York still couldn't win a World Series. Once more Ruppert prevailed on "Frazz," as he now chummily called him, this time for Herb Pennock, a stylish left hander, and George Pipgras, a promising youngster. Pipgras did not bloom in New York until 1928 (24 victories), but Pennock took to the big town immediately. "The Squire of Kennett Square" contributed two wins to the Yankees' World Series triumph in 1923. Of the 24 world champion Yankees, 11 were from Boston.

In 1923, Reach's *Baseball Guide* reported: "Boston's last season reaped the fruits of four years' despoliation by the New York club, and for the second time in American League history this once great Boston team, now utterly discredited, fell into last place—with every prospect of remaining in that undesirable position indefinitely."

When Frazee died in his New York apartment in 1929, James J. Walker, mayor of New York, was at his bedside, no doubt to honor a man who had done as much for New York sports as anyone. The Red Sox didn't begin to recover from the Frazee-induced hemorrhage until Tom Yawkey arrived with his open checkbook in 1933.

What was the reaction of the stars who were traded? When Ruth was first told, he was visibly irritated. "My heart is in Boston; I have a farm in Sudbury." Then he received his contract from the Yankees— $20,000 a year for two years—and his opinion of Beantown soured. "Well, that Frazee was pretty cheap anyway," said the Babe. "They had a Babe Ruth Day for me last year and I had to buy my wife's ticket to the game. Fifteen thousand fans show up and all I got was a cigar."

Two more of Harry Frazee's boner trades. *Opposite top:* Herb Pennock, "the Squire of Kennett Square." *Opposite bottom:* Joe Dugan, one of the few good players Frazee actually received in trade. He lasted half a season in Boston.

The Coming of Tom Yawkey (interview)

In 1933, Thomas Austin Yawkey bought a debt-ridden baseball team from Bob Quinn and the Winslow estate. The purchase brought to an end a period in Red Sox history that can be described as "Quinn's Weather"—that dire time in the late twenties and early thirties when the Depression put the final nail in the coffin of Bob's ventures in sports. Quinn had been the driving force in shaping the 1922 Browns, the best American League team St. Louis had ever had, but baseball sage that he was, Quinn could not build the Red Sox into a winner. Quinn himself mused, "Every time we get ready for a big crowd, it seems to rain. They even have an expression around here if it rains. They say, 'Well, here comes Quinn's Weather'."

By 1933, the rain had become a deluge; if Quinn had not sold out then, there is an excellent chance that he would have gone bankrupt. His and the Red Sox' savior was Tom Yawkey, a wealthy sportsman who wanted to build a ball club—precisely the sort of buyer to whom Quinn felt he could entrust his beloved but fast-failing Sox. The transaction was made, and Quinn gracefully yielded to a man somewhat less knowledgeable than he about the baseball business but every bit as enthusiastic.

As expected, Yawkey paid the debts and renovated the Red Sox' stadium, Fenway Park, which was already more than 20 years old. Then, aided by the brilliant Eddie Collins, whom he had insisted upon hiring as his general manager, Yawkey took the initiative; he opened

his checkbook and scoured the league for fresh talent.

The first acquisitions of the new Boston management were catcher Rick Ferrell and shortly afterward, his pitching brother, Wes. The pair provided the Red Sox with a first-rate battery as well as a family unit. From Philadelphia's Connie Mack, Yawkey procured Lefty Grove and a few years later Jimmie Foxx, but these were only the Hall of Famers. Among the others of a host of Athletics who came to Boston in the thirties were Rube Walberg, Max Bishop, Bing Miller, Doc Cramer, Louis Finney, Eric McNair, Mike ("Pinky") Higgins, and Dib Williams.

Yawkey's most expensive single acquisition was Joe Cronin, from Senators owner Clark Griffith. For a quarter of a million dollars, Yawkey brought to Boston a man who would play an immensely important part in the Red Sox' organization for nearly a quarter century, from 1935 until 1959, when he became president of the American League.

But despite the money Yawkey doled out for talent, the nucleus of his pennant winners and near pennant winners consisted of players the Red Sox developed themselves: Bobby Doerr, Dom DiMaggio, Tex Hughson, Johnny Pesky, Boo Ferriss, Mel Parnell, and Vern Stephens in the late thirties and forties; Jim Lonborg, Rico Petrocelli, Tony Conigliaro, and George Scott in the sixties; and, of course, the two biggest Red Sox superstars, Ted Williams and his successor, Carl Yastrzemski.

The man who has attended so assiduously to the business of developing a winner has not gone financially unrewarded for his efforts. Again in 1974, his team led the American League in attendance, though it

Opposite top and bottom: Yawkey at contract time with his two superstars, Williams and Yastrzemski. *Above:* Perhaps the best (certainly the most expensive) deal Yawkey ever made—Cronin for Lyn Lary and $250,000.

21

trailed in the standings and continued to play in a park that seats fewer fans than any other American League stadium. The 1.6 million attendance for 1974 compared to 181,000 in the last pre-Yawkey year gives some indication of his success.

The most persistent criticism of Yawkey has been: "He's too soft on the players." Perhaps it's true. Certainly he is far more considerate of his players than several other franchise owners are of theirs. He has even been patronizing to the employees. But for those who would blame Yawkey's treatment of his players for the Sox' heartbreaks in 1948, 1949, 1950, 1972, and 1974, it might be well to remember that his attitude in those years was not noticeably different than it was in 1946 or 1967.

You have now been a major league club owner longer than anyone else ever. How did this all come about?

Well first, the Red Sox were available. Bob Quinn and a man named Winslow had bought the team. Then Winslow died. They were in debt to everyone. Ty Cobb had introduced me to Eddie Collins several years before. Collins had gone to the same prep school I had, and we used to occasionally have dinner together. One night Collins said, "You love the game; why don't you look into the Red Sox? I know Quinn will sell it to the right man." I guess I was the right man.

You said the team was in debt. How bad was it?

It was bad. I had to pay off [Harry M.] Stevens, the concessionaire. Then there was the league; the Red Sox owed a hundred and fifty thousand dollars to the American League. I remember the first meeting I at-

tended. Old Walter Briggs [owner of the Detroit Tigers] opened the session with, "I know the Yawkey family. They've got money. I don't think the league should be a bank." He did know my family; my father's estate had sold our Tiger stock to Walter O. [Briggs] and Mr. [John] Kelsey. Well, I told Mr. [Will] Harridge [the American League President] all right and I wrote out another check.

Any other debts?

Yes, and I'll tell you a funny story. There was still the demand mortgage that Harry Frazee had put through Jake Ruppert. I went to the Colonel and told him I had already laid out a great deal of cash, and I wondered if he could carry the mortgage into the following year. He said yes, he was delighted to have me in the league.

Well, that season [1933] the Yankees came into Fenway and we swept them five straight. The next morning my lawyer in New York called to say it was a costly sweep. Ruppert's lawyer had just called, and they were demanding payment right now on the mortgage. Jake didn't like to lose five straight. So I sent the SOB [laughter] a check the next day.

One of the first things you did was bring Eddie Collins in as general manager.

Eddie was a tremendous student of the game, as good as *anyone* ever was, and better than the overwhelming majority. I had the opportunity of sitting with Eddie for a good many years; there was always something going on out on the field for Eddie. He was as patient as hell with me explaining the subtleties of the game. He's the one who built our team of forty-six.

One of Yawkey's home-grown products was Bobby Doerr, the anchor of the Boston infield during his 14 years in the majors—all of them with the Red Sox.

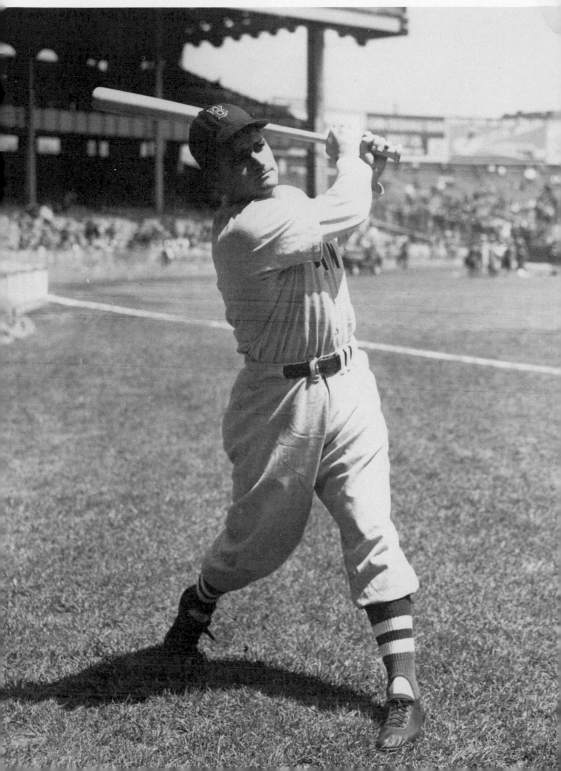

The Joe Cronin deal was the most expensive in baseball up to that time. In purchasing power those two hundred and fifty thousand dollars in 1935 were probably as sizable as the inflated figures today.

It was Collins' suggestion. I was at a league meeting with Griff—he was a wonderful man—and I said, "What will you take for Cronin?" Griff came back with, "Why, he's just married Mildred" [Griffith's niece]. I asked him what that had to do with his playing shortstop. Griff replied, "Oh, I couldn't sell Joe." Then the meeting got going for about an hour when Griff whispered, "I'd want too much money for him anyway."

I answered, "Well, put your figure down on the back of this envelope and see."

He did and came back with, "Of course I won't have anybody to play shortstop, so you'll have to throw in Lyn Lary."

His figure was two hundred and fifty thousand dollars and so I said, "Okay, that's it."

What has been your brightest moment since you came to Boston?

Oh, I guess it has to be those two games against Minnesota in sixty-seven [see pages 86-96]. The pennant-winning years are, of course, the greatest and sixty-seven was more so than forty-six. We knew we had a contending team in forty-six, and then when we won all those games at the beginning, it became a runaway [see pages 70-79]. In sixty-seven, on the other hand, we had to fight all the way, and winning it then has to be my greatest thrill. Conversely, those two games at the end of the season in forty-nine have to be my keenest disappointment [see pages 80-84]. I wish we hadn't been forced to use both [Ellis] Kinder and

[Mel] Parnell in relief in those games in Washington, especially Mel. With a little more rest I honestly think Parnell could have beaten the Yankees the first game at the stadium.

Can you think of any one player you wish you had not traded?

You can never tell when you make a trade if it's going to work out or not. You just can't get value without giving value in return. Of course, while I don't make the deals, if it's a big one, they'll call and ask my opinion. [General manager] Dick O'Connell called me in seventy-one and said, "We're about to make a multiplayer deal with Milwaukee. Do you have any suggestions?"

I said, "Hell, you haven't got a lead-off man—get [Tommy] Harper. He can steal and he can hit with power."

Well, goddamn, you want one player I wish we hadn't traded. I'll say young [Lynn] McGlothen. He's going to be quite a pitcher before he's through in the game.

What are the future plans for Fenway Park?

We've kicked that around for years. I went through that with [former governor of Massachusetts John] Volpe so many times. The days when an individual can build a stadium on his own are long gone. We'll be in Fenway for some years to come as far as I'm concerned. Remember, we don't have any football here to cut up the field. I think our field is as good or better than any in baseball.

I'd like to make out a twenty-five-man squad of your years with the Red Sox. How about opening up with three catchers, Rick Ferrell, Birdie Tebbetts, and Carlton Fisk?

I'd have to agree with that.

Slugging first baseman Jimmie Foxx came to the Red Sox in 1936. He was sold by Philadelphia's Connie Mack, from whom, it was said, Yawkey tried "to buy a pennant."

An infield of Foxx at first, Doerr at second, Cronin at short, and [Frank] Malzone at third?

Offhand, you can't argue with that.

My three spare infielders are Petrocelli, Stephens, and Pesky?

Rico, Vern, and "Needle"—very good, terriffic, you've given this a lot of thought.

This outfield seems set, Williams, Yaz, and DiMaggio?

Ted, "Yamstramski" [T. A. likes to pronounce it that way], and D. D. —a terriffic analysis.

How about these for the three spare outfielders, [Jackie] Jensen, Cramer, and Tony C.?

Yes, well they were strong players. We've had some streak players— Clyde Volmer and Carl Reynolds are two that come to mind. One year [1951], Volmer had six great weeks; they couldn't get him out. Reynolds used to hit four hundred each year until the first of June. Then he would tail off.

Jensen was good for a whole year —maybe it was his football background. It took a big injury to get him out. Jackie was one player who used all the tools he had to the best of his ability; he always gave you a hundred percent. Doc Cramer was the same; one year there he played in every game we had.

Here are my pitchers: Tex Hughson, Mel Parnell, Luis Tiant, Ellis Kinder, Wes Ferrell, Lefty Grove, Jim Lonborg, and Dick Radatz. I have included Radatz because I think in sixty-three and sixty-four he was the best relief pitcher Boston ever had.

Certainly—on Radatz. You didn't have [Dave ("Boo")] Ferriss, did you? He has to be there. In forty-six he was sensational, the real difference on that team. And he won twenty for us in forty-five. Of course, the hitting wasn't great that year. I remember saying I'd pay the price of admission just to watch Ted Williams come back for batting practice. Dave was a splendid competitor. He was also a tremendously fine person.

What do you think of the chances of the team in the future?

We have these two kids, Jim Rice and Freddy Lynn. Honestly, I've watched them and I can't see how they can miss. We drafted Rice out of high school, but we just got Lynn out of USC a year ago last June. Rice has been a star for us wherever he's been. He is certainly ready. Lynn has come as fast as anybody I've ever seen this season [1974]. We're going to have to find room for them for years to come.

Above: Yawkey's Fenway during first night game, June 16, 1947. *Opposite:* one of the more versatile stars from the Yawkey era, former football great Jackie Jensen. *Left:* "the Monster," reliever Dick Radatz.

The Changing of the Guard

Ted Williams' career spanned more than one baseball era. He saw the end of the long train rides, the emergence and then dominance of night ball, the development of the relief specialist, and the coming of the black player. He batted against Red Ruffing, Ted Lyons, and Bobo Newsome. He was there when Lefty Grove won his three hundredth and when Jimmie Foxx hit his five hundredth. In a later, considerably less glorious time, he watched Jimmy Piersall shoot off his water pistols and Pumpsie Green (the Red Sox' first black player) play his first game. In 1939, Ted homered off left hander Thornton Lee. In 1960, he homered off right hander Don Lee, Thornton's son. He came to the majors when the world stood on the brink of war and left when being on the brink of war had become commonplace.

No mere observer, he marked the changing eras. In the spring training camp of 1938, the kid from San Diego stood next to Bobby Doerr, and the second baseman said, "Ted, wait till you see Foxx hit."

Williams was alleged to have answered, "Wait till Foxx sees me hit."

He was hounded by criticism yet defiant of it. "Why doesn't Ted go in the service?" critics asked in 1942, though they never questioned Joe DiMaggio or Stan Musial, who didn't enter the navy until 1945. The criticism hardly abated when Williams took the field. The chief Williams bater, "Colonel" Egan of the Boston *Daily Record,* wrote an article in which he claimed that the Red Sox didn't win because Ted received too many walks. Swinging only at good

Opposite top: jesting with Foxx. *Right:* facing Feller. Note shortstop positioned behind pitcher—part of the infield shift that became a common defense against Ted's pull hitting.

pitches, getting on base, and scoring runs (if it were not for his military service, Ted would have scored more than any other player in history) were not what critics considered good enough for the superstar of a team often stocked with mediocrity.

The day he quit (after having played in parts of four decades) baseball did its best to forget the less triumphant parts of his career, but at first it wasn't easy to be festive. The last day Ted Williams played major league baseball—September 26, 1960, in Fenway Park —was as dark and dismal a day as the entire 1960 season had been for the Sox. Billy Jurges had been fired as manager in midseason. Pinky Higgins had returned to replace him, but the team had not improved. Only the bumbling Kansas City Athletics (with first baseman

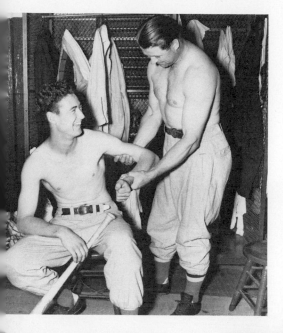

Marv Throneberry, who would reach his pinnacle of ineptness with the Mets) had saved the Red Sox from last place.

One of the few pleasant things about 1960 had been the attendance. More than 1.1 million fans had paid their way into Fenway, the last time the Sox would pass a million until the pennant-winning year of 1967. Just as the aging Babe Ruth had attracted fans to the Yankees in 1934 for a last look at the great home run hitter, so Williams brought forth the fans for whom he had come to symbolize baseball in Boston. Corny as it may have been, middle-aged fathers wanted their sons to be able to say they had seen Ted Williams play.

By and large the fans had not been disappointed. His efforts as an outfielder had become painful to watch

(he chased a fly ball as gracelessly as a wounded buffalo limping to a water hole), but at the plate the 42-year-old slugger was still formidable. He may not have quite reached his goal of being the best hitter who ever lived, but in 1960, he was still tenaciously close to the top, batting .316 and hitting a home run almost every ten times at bat.

Eleven thousand fans had come to see this final game at Boston in 1960 in order to bid adieu to Williams. Their hero would reward them with one of the most triumphantly dramatic moments in the history of baseball.

As all such occasions do, this one opened with a ceremony. Everybody extolled Williams. The Sox retired his number "9" and presented him with a silver bowl, a plaque, and a $4,000 check for the Jimmy Fund, the children's charity Williams had long supported. Then they gave the mike to Williams. "Despite some of the terrible things written about me by the knights of the keyboard up there," he began, "and they were terrible things —I'd like to forget them but I can't— my stay in Boston has been the most wonderful part of my life. If someone should ask me the one place I'd want to play if I had it to do all over again, I would say Boston, for it has the greatest owner in baseball and the greatest fans in America."

Steve Barber started the game for the visiting Orioles, but he walked the first three batters, including Ted, and was promptly yanked in favor of Jack Fisher, another member of Baltimore's "kiddie corps" of 1960.

The aging Williams blasts a home run against the Washington Senators on opening day, 1960, his last season.

30

(Jack Fisher was born while Williams was in spring training in 1939.) Ted faced Fisher in the third inning and flied to Jackie Brandt in deep center.

In the fifth it looked as if Ted really had a home run. He sent one high and deep toward the bullpen, but Al Pilarcik stayed with it and made the catch with his back against the fence. Williams loped into the dugout, turned to Vic Wertz, and lamented, "If that one didn't go out, none of them will today."

By the seventh inning a rumor started to sweep through the stands. "This is really it; Ted's not going to Yankee Stadium for the final series of the year," the fans whispered. They sensed that this would indeed be Ted's last game as a Red Sox, and they were right. Before the game, the aging, aching slugger had confided to manager Higgins that he wanted to play no more.

As Ted walked to the plate in the eighth, the crowd rose as one in a thunderous ovation that said good-bye to this man and the era he represented. The cheering was also a gesture of encouragement for a man who finally looked as if he might need some—a 22-year veteran (now affectionately called "Shad Belly" by owner Yawkey) facing a 21-year-old fireballer who wanted to strike him out.

The dampness had become uncomfortable. (The lights had been turned on, revealing a light drizzle.) Fisher's first pitch came in high for a ball. "Oh, Christ, don't walk him," someone moaned. The fear vanished as Ted took an unsuccessful cut at a shoulder-high fastball on the outside corner of the plate.

Fisher then made a fatal mistake; he tried the same pitch again. This time the classic swing met the ball and sent it rocketing toward the distant right-center field bleachers.

Every person in Fenway but one went berserk. Ted calmly circled the bases for his five hundred and twenty-first home run, returned to the dugout, and stayed there through a prolonged roar by the faithful for a curtain call. He had thanked the fans in his farewell speech, and that would have to do. In the top of the ninth, Higgins sent him out to left field, then immediately replaced him with Carroll Hardy. As he ran into the dugout, Ted still did not acknowledge the crowd with a tip of the hat. Williams was not about to break any habits on his last day, and in retrospect, perhaps he can be better appreciated for it.

The next morning one of the Boston writers stated: "Let's face it, what are we going to write about now?" The man to fill the void was a young Long Island potato farmer, then burning up the American Association with 193 hits. (In 1938, the young Williams had himself collected 193 hits in the same league.) Carl Yastrzemski would take over left field in 1961 and, after a slow start, develop into the team leader, a status he still retains. Yaz does not dominate the Sox as Ted did (especially in the post-Korean War period), but he has come close. Together, the two left fielders have been an overpowering influence on the Red Sox for 35 years: Ted, the prewar superstar who played in four decades for Boston, and Carl, the star of an era in which every team takes pride in having at least one player in the six-figure salary class.

As symbolic as any play on the field can be, Williams' home run in his final appearance at the plate signaled the changing of the guard. Rarely has a superstar yielded his mantle of leadership as fittingly.

The Future Is Young

In March 1974, Boston manager Darrell Johnson released shortstop Luis Aparicio, designated hitter Orlando Cepeda, and relief pitcher Bob Bolin. They were all well into their thirties, and this was to be the year the Red Sox would thrive on youth. It didn't quite work out that way. Backstop Carlton Fisk, rookie of the year in 1972 and the backbone of the rebuilding program, injured a leg on June 28 in a collision at the plate and was lost for the season. His replacement, Bob Montgomery, in one stretch threw out eight of nine runners attempting to steal—one of the few bright spots in the great decline of 1974 and a refutation of those who said his arm was weak—but Fisk was still sorely missed. Two other mainstays of the youth movement, Dwight ("Dewey") Evans in right field and Doug Griffin at second base, were lost for substantial periods through injury. Then late in the year the Red Sox picked up 36-year-old Deron Johnson, and young Jim Rice, who had just finished devastating the International League, sat on the bench. On September 12, the lineup that was to have emphasized youth included Tommy Harper, 34, in left; Rico Petrocelli, 31, at third; Dick McAuliffe, 33, at short; Montgomery, 30, behind the plate; and Johnson as designated hitter.

As the youth movement fizzled, so did the preseason hope for a running ball club. Only still-sprightly Tommy Harper stole more than 20 bases. The best the rest could do was a nifty double-steal routine that petered out with everything else in the second half of the year.

Not as young nor as fast as they had hoped to. be, the Red Sox none-

One of the youngsters who is becoming a fixture at Fenway, second baseman Doug Griffin. Here he pivots against Twins.

33

theless led the American League's East Division by as much as seven games in August. But this was the year of the great flopperoo, a great year turned sour. Never before has a Red Sox team blown a pennant after having been as far in front as this one was as late in the year.

The swoon hit on a nine-game road trip at the end of August. The Sox won two of three from Chicago, then lost a 3-2 decision to Bert Blyleven at Minnesota, though the Twins presented them with two unearned runs in the fourth inning. The next day they earned two runs but lost anyway. Then on September 1, for one of the few times all year, they blew a big lead. Ahead 6-2 in the seventh, Johnson brought in Diego Segui to replace Reggie Cleveland, but the number-one reliever was as effective as a parasol in a hurricane. The crushing shot was a three-run homer by a .217-hitting spare first baseman from Worcester, Massachusetts, Pat Bourque.

Reeling from the disastrous three days in Minnesota, the Sox arrived in Baltimore to be met by the Orioles' best, Mike Cuellar, Ross Grimsley, and Jim Palmer. Boston went scoreless in 27 innings and dropped another three straight. Thus, in one short week, the Bosox had virtually dissipated what had once been a commanding lead. Mathematically, the flag was still far from lost. But this proved to be the slip that began the landslide. Mired in a dreadful hitting slump, the Red Sox made a September ritual of moving runners into scoring position with less than two outs, only to strand them. Meanwhile, both the Orioles and Yankees played superbly in the last month of the season, delivering the timely hits and doing everything else pennant winners do.

Opposite: the star of the new generation until his injury in 1974, Carlton Fisk. *Above:* Cecil Cooper takes a tumble.

Shortstop Rick ("Rooster") Burleson avoids Dick Allen and guns to first.

Clockwise from below: Dwight ("Dewey")
Evans scores against Royals; Yaz unloads
against Oakland; Beniquez caps first
big league grand slammer; manager Darrell
Johnson with elderly DH, Deron Johnson.

And so once again the Red Sox
finished the season resolutely looking forward to the next one to as-
suage their disappointment. And once
again the team pinned its hopes
mostly on the young players who
were supposed to have revived it in
1974. In the outfield Dewey Evans,
Juan Beniquez, Rick Miller, and newcomers Jim Rice and Fred Lynn may
make it difficult for veterans Harper
and Bernie Carbo to make the team
in 1975 (if they are not traded for
bullpen help before then). [Ed. note:
in December Harper was traded to
California for infielder Bob Heise.]
At 22, Evans has already established
himself as a bona fide major leaguer
with an arm that hasn't been
matched in right field at Fenway

since Harry Hooper of the Golden Outfield. Miller and Beniquez in center are both quite fast, though Miller's bat and Beniquez's glove are still in question. Fred Lynn produced a miraculous spurt when he arrived from Pawtucket in mid-September, and there is no question that Boston is counting on him for left field in 1975. He went 8 for 14 in a four-game stretch, including a triple, a double, and two singles in five at-bats against Detroit on the eighteenth. Then, on his very next time up the next evening, he homered. Rice has gained equally impressive notices. He not only won the Triple Crown at Pawtucket in 1974 but led the Eastern League in hitting with Bristol the year before, then graduated at season's end to Pawtucket (managed by Darrell Johnson) and helped the team to victory in the Junior World Series.

In the infield, too, the Sox abound with youngsters: Cecil Cooper as a backup to Yaz and part-time DH, Griffin at second, Rick Burleson and Mario Guerrero at short, and at third possibly Terry Hughes to replace Petrocelli, who has spoken of retirement. And if Carlton Fisk can come back—a big if—the new generation will have its star.

Other than its ace, Luis Tiant, 34, the pitching staff is almost as young as the rest of the team. Left hander Bill Lee completed another fine year, which would have been even better had he not been victimized by 1-0

losses to Baltimore on Labor Day and to New York on September 25. Nevertheless, he notched his fourth consecutive winning season with Boston—quite a feat for a southpaw.

The third starter is the enigmatic Rogelio Moret, at 25 still young enough to realize the promise he has shown. The fourth is Dick Drago, who arrived from Kansas City in 1974 and did not show the form with which he won 17 games for the Royals in 1971 but is still a viable complement to Tiant, Lee, and Moret. Reggie Cleveland is the fifth starter and long relief man; Diego Segui is the heart of a bullpen that needs bolstering. Rick Wise's shoulder leaves his future in doubt, and Steve Pole, of the Pawtucket shuttle, has been predictable only in his inconsistency. Steve Barr had a strong year at Bristol and pitched a steady if not sensational game against Cleveland after the race had been decided. It is a long but not unprecedented jump from the Eastern League to the majors.

The 1974 season was not the first one in which Boston fans were disappointed after having been primed to expect a new, youthful, running team. For 1975, the indomitable hope of rejuvenation rises again. With only two of 1967's Impossible Dreamers left (Yaz and Rico), the time is overdue for the new generation to revive the memories of Williams and Yastrzemski triumphant.

123456789

GREAT YEARS

1903

Honus, why do you hit so badly,
Take a back seat and sit down.
Honus, at bat you look so sadly.
Hey, why don't you get out of town.

—sung by the Royal Rooters to the tune of
"Tessie" at the first World Series

In 1903, the American League came of age. A mere two years after its founding, it not only won temporary recognition from the 28-year-old National League but also defeated the senior circuit in the first World Series, the symbol of the two leagues' new accord. The American League's victory was one of baseball's greatest upsets. The team responsible for it, the team that raised Ban Johnson's infant league to instant maturity, was the Boston Pilgrims, the property of one Henry Killilea, a Milwaukee lawyer. Killilea bought the club from its original owner, Arthur Somers, the American League's financial sprinkler, who in 1903 realized he had been whirling too fast and loose with his assets and decided to consolidate instead.

It was perhaps unkind that crass financial affairs prevented Somers from presiding over the Pilgrims' greening, but world championships are not won on sentiment, as the Pilgrims demonstrated on opening day in taking the first game of a doubleheader from the Philadelphia Athletics. After Philly manager Connie Mack announced that the great hurler and boozer, Rube Waddell, would be his starting pitcher, Boston's player-manager, Jimmy Collins, called his team together for a strategy session. "Boys," Jimmy told his charges, "the Rube has just come off a tremendous bender. We're going to bunt the hell out of him—run his

arse all over the park." Following instructions perfectly, the Pilgrims further befuddled the already soused Waddell and won 9-4.

In the second game, Mack unveiled a 19-year-old Chippewa Indian, Chief Bender, who stopped the Pilgrims cold. Thus, Boston ended its first day of the season at .500, a record they would maintain for the next two months. In June and July they started to improve and in August they turned the race into a romp. With a league-leading team batting average of .292 and mound stars Cy Young (28-9), Big Bill Dineen (21-13), and Tom Hughes

The 1903 Pilgrims on the bench during the World Series. At far left is Cy Young.

(20-7), they finished 14½ games ahead of Philadelphia.

The Pilgrims' slugger was Buck Freeman, an outfielder who, playing for Washington when it was in the National League, had established the all-time one-season home run record of 25. He hit only 13 in 1903, but it was enough to lead the American League and a respectable total even by today's inflated standards for a man who stood 5 feet 9 inches and weighed 150 pounds. Freeman wasn't the only man ever to lead both leagues in circuit clouts, but he certainly was the smallest.

Another outfielder, Patsy Dough-erty, led the team in batting with a .331 average. Chick Stahl, the third outfielder, had an off year at .274.

The infield was composed of Candy LaChance at first, Hobe Ferris and Freddy Parent up the middle, and Collins himself at third. Although LaChance was almost at the end of the road, the other three gave the Pilgrims a stellar defense in an era when fielding dominated the game. Lou Criger, who had been Cy Young's catcher in the National League, and Chick Stahl's kid brother, Garland, covered the catching. Garland would later be nicknamed Jake and lead the Red Sox to glory on his own.

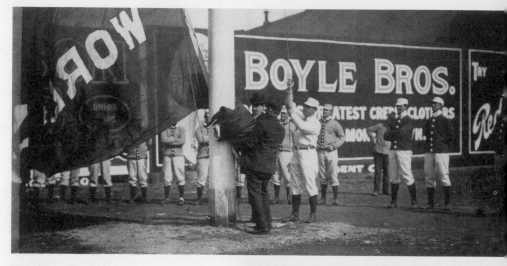

The World Series

When it became obvious in August that the Pilgrims would win the American League pennant, baseball fans and writers began clamoring for a postseason playoff between the winners in both leagues. Finally the two leagues agreed; the winners of each pennant would meet in a best-of-nine series when the regular season ended.

"We can beat the Giants and that loudmouth McGraw, or the Pirates no matter how good Wagner is," boasted the patrons of McGreevey's saloon. Mr. McGreevey, the proprietor, confidently raised his hands and intoned, "Enough said,"—thus earning the nickname, "Nuff Ced". This saloon was the spawning ground for the Royal Rooters, the Pilgrims' fast-developing fan club that would make a tradition of gathering at McGreevey's to sing the glories of its ball team.

But as far as the oddsmakers were concerned, the Rooters were just whistling Dixie. Buttressed by a strong pitching staff (from June 2 to

Top: flag being raised at first World Series. *Right:* Bill Dineen, hatless in foreground, confronts Pittsburgh cop. *Far right:* outfielder Chick Stahl.

8 it had recorded six consecutive shutout victories), the great Honus Wagner at short, player-manager Fred Clarke in left field, and the mighty mite, Tommy Leach, at third, the Pirates were the overwhelming favorite to defeat Boston. The experts concluded that the Bucs would not even miss one of their star pitchers, Ed Doheny, who had been committed as a homicidal maniac (he tried to strangle a nurse) late in the season.

"Who are they going to beat us with—that old farmer, Cy Young?" jeered the Pirates. "We chased him out of our league. Or Bill Dineen? He could never beat us when he was with the [National League Boston] Beaneaters."

Barney Dreyfuss, the Pirates' owner, arrived for the first game at the Huntington Avenue grounds in Boston convinced his Bucs would win a short series. He was piqued when the Boston management forced him to buy a ticket ("Imagine, making me pay to see my own team play!"), but he recovered his composure when the Pirates' Deacon Phillippe handcuffed the Pilgrims 7-3. Cy Young started for Boston and allowed 12 hits, including two triples by Leach and the first World Series home run—by a banjo hitter, Jimmy Sebring.

The next day Bill Dineen silenced the Pirates' bats and mouths with a 3-0 shutout. Boston's big gun was

45

the amiable Celt, Patsy Dougherty, who endeared himself to Boston fans with two home runs. ("We love yuh, Patsy darlin'!")

Then Boston's fortunes turned sour. With an assist from the weatherman, Deacon Phillippe beat Boston twice more—once in Boston and then, after two days of rainstorms, in Pittsburgh. The first was a 4-2 victory over Tom Hughes, the second a 5-4 triumph over Dineen. Phillippe had now beaten the Pilgrims three times in the first four games, after which the jubilant Pittsburgh fans marched all over the field with the Deacon on their shoulders.

The 100 Royal Rooters who had accompanied their heroes on the trip to Pittsburgh were suddenly silent, and their compatriots at home now had to endure the taunts of the Boston National League fans. "Collins has a nice team, but now he's playing in the big leagues again," they jeered. It was the last sneering they would do for a long time.

Down 3-1 in games, Collins called on Young to stop the Pirates, and the Farmer responded, holding the Pirates to four hits in an 11-2 victory. Before the game a delegation of Pittsburgh fans had marched over to the Royal Rooters' section. Handing a large many-hued umbrella to Nuff Ced, they quipped, "Here, Mr. McGreevey, you'll need this to ward off our base hits."

McGreevey laughed and graciously accepted the bumbershoot, but added, "We may make a few of our own, don't you know." Then, as the Pilgrims shelled the Pirates, Nuff Ced danced a jig on the Boston dugout waving the large umbrella at the Pirates—the first known voodoo dance in baseball.

46

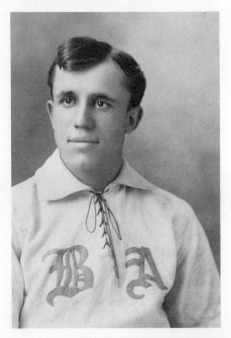

Clockwise from left: shortstop Fred Parent; Royal Rooters singing(?) "Tessie" to brass band accompaniment during Series (note umbrellas near top left); frenzied partisan exhorts the fans.

Heroes of 1903 meet years later:
left, Big Bill Dineen, then an
umpire, and "the Farmer," Cy Young.

Big Bill evened the Series in the sixth game, besting Sam Leever 6-3. "It was that goddamn song 'Tessie' that band of theirs was always playing," wailed Tommy Leach. "It was driving us nuts." Tommy should have known. The usually flawless third baseman made a wild throw in the third that allowed Boston three runs.

With the Series tied at three games each, Dreyfuss intervened to ensure that Phillippe would be fresh for the pivotal seventh game, the

last one in Pittsburgh. The Pittsburgh owner said it was too cold to play on Friday, the ninth, as scheduled, so he postponed the game until Saturday. The weather was no better the next day, but apparently Dreyfuss thought his star pitcher had had enough rest.

A surge of extra fans forced the Pittsburgh management to rope off part of the outfield, creating a ground-rule triple area that the Red Sox found attractive. They clouted five of them into the crowd in beating Phillippe for the first time, 7-3. Pittsburgh was stunned. Boston had taken three straight, and the Pirates hadn't really been close in any of

them. The Bucs now faced the unattractive task of winning two straight in Boston against the surging Pilgrims and their ecstatic allies, the Royal Rooters. "Didn't the Farmer handle the Dutchman [Honus Wagner]," chirped Freddy Parent. (Wagner had gone 0 for 11 in the last three games.)

Rain and cold weather delayed the Series for two days when the teams reached Boston. It wasn't until October 13, some two weeks after the Series had begun, that they played what became the final game. On this cold, raw day, Big Bill beat the durable Deacon and Pittsburgh for the clincher, 3-0. The American League Pilgrims had won and had at least temporarily rid themselves of the disdain of the Nationals. The next year the interleague strife erupted again, and the 1904 American League champion Pilgrims did not have a chance to play for the world championship. But by 1905, the two leagues had learned to peacefully coexist, and the World Series resumed.

A further postscript to the first World Series was the reaction of the owners. Dreyfuss was crushed. When the winners' share was announced as $1,182 a player, the man who before the Series had said, "I've only done this so my boys would make a little extra money," immediately called his Pirates together. "You did a great job," he acknowledged. "I'm not going to make a dime out of this; I'm turning the owner's share over to you." Thus, the vanquished team ended up with $1,316 a player —more than the victors.

There was none of the *noblesse oblige* about Killilea. He promptly sold out, thus setting a still-standing major league record for the quickest disposition of a world champion.

1912

"Can I throw harder than Joe Wood? Listen, my friend, there's no man alive can throw harder than Smoky Joe Wood."

—Walter Johnson

This was a year that began with changes and ended with coups. First, the Red Sox' management changed hands, at least in part, then the field manager was replaced, then the team moved into a new ball park. Then the revamped Bostonians toppled the world champion Philadelphia Athletics by winning the American League crown, and finally, in the very last inning of the last game of the World Series, aided and abetted the self-destruction of the New York Giants.

A key figure in the change of ownership was American League President Ban Johnson, no stranger to baseball wars, even when they were supposedly the internal affairs of sovereign clubs. In 1912, General Charles Taylor, the successor to Henry Killilea as owner of the Boston Pilgrims and the man who in 1907 changed the team's name to "Red Sox," put 50 percent of the club up for sale. Johnson induced him to sell to a group headed by a former journeyman outfielder, Jimmy Mc-Aleer, and one of Johnson's colleagues, Bob McKay, secretary of the American League. The new regime purged manager Patsy Donovan, who was given to sanctimonious piety, which McAleer found distasteful. Patsy was replaced by Jake Stahl, a grubbier sort who had married a banker's daughter in 1910, retired from baseball, and spent his days counting deposits for his father-in-law before the new management lured him back to the ball field with an offer to play first base and manage.

With their household in order, the Red Sox now found a new home for it at Landsdowne and Jersey Streets on the property of the Fenway Realty Company, whose largest stockholder was, to no one's surprise, the very same General Taylor who had just relieved himself of the command of the ball club. The new ball park followed the vogue for steel and concrete that Philadelphia with Shibe Park and Pittsburgh with Forbes Field had begun in 1909. Although Tom Yawkey rebuilt much of it in 1934, Fenway Park remains today essentially the same as it was at its birth more than 60 years ago. Its most famous characteristic, of course, is the 37-foot-high wall, which extends from the foul pole in left (315 feet from home plate) to the flagpole (388 feet from home), well past left center. Many fly balls that would have been caught had they been hit in another park have landed in the screen atop the wall (a home run) or bounced off the wall for base hits. On the other hand many line drives that would have carried out of other parks have failed to clear Fenway's wall. The spacious right field (only 302 feet down the line but 380 feet in straightaway right) is a further disadvantage to the power hitter. Before the bullpens were constructed in front of the right center field bleachers to aid Ted Williams, the distance to straightaway right was more than 400 feet.

For the ball players Fenway is at best idiosyncratic, at worst a travesty of a ball park. But for the spectators it is a delight. It is so small (capacity is only 33,379) that almost every fan is close to the field. There is no better place to watch a ball game.

The team that opened the new park with a 7-6 win over the New York Highlanders was not expected to overtake the Philadelphia Athletics for the pennant. Athletics manager Connie Mack later moaned, "I still think my team of 1912 was my best of that era, but Wood kept winning those games." He was referring to Joe Wood, a 22-year-old product of the plains of Kansas and the mining towns of Colorado who could throw a baseball through a two-by-four. Against hitters armed only with bats, he won 34 games in 1912 and lost only 5. No major leaguer has since won more.

Wood's chief assistants on the mound staff were Bucky O'Brien and Hughie Bedient, both of whom pitched better in 1912 than they ever would again. Having been raised in nearby Brockton, Massachusetts, O'Brien was the darling of the Irish who had been immigrating to the Boston area since the potato famine of the 1840s. His mainstay was the then-legal spitball, which helped him to 19 wins in 1912. The next year he was 4-9 and out of the league. Bedient was a 22-year-old rookie from upstate New York who lasted a bit longer. He put together a record of 18-9 in 1912, but by 1915, he too was out of the majors.

Both Ray Collins and Charlie ("Sea Lion") Hall contributed 15 wins. The stylish, left-handed Collins was young and just beginning to perfect the form that would make him a 20-

game winner in 1913 and 1914. But for the veteran Sea Lion, 1912 was the last bark.

Thus, five pitchers—Wood, O'Brien, Bedient, Collins, and Hall—contributed 101 of the Sox' 105 wins (a Boston team record), all but overshadowing one Benjamin Harrison Van Dyke, whose name is better remembered than his modest contribution as a pitcher—1 win.

With help from rookie Forrest Cady, Bill Carrigan handled the catching. Carrigan was the archetype of the brainy catcher of the period, who often compensated for lack of talent with fierce aggressiveness and an uncanny knowledge of the game. His particular talents were soon to be even better displayed.

In the three years from 1914–16, he would manage the Red Sox to two world championships.

Jake Stahl at first and Larry Gardner at third gave the team .300 hitters at the corners. Second baseman Steve Yerkes and veteran shortstop Heinie Wagner, neither one a threat at the plate, nevertheless gave excellent protection up the middle.

The outfield was Golden. As a unit, Duffy Lewis in left, Tris Speaker In center, and Harry Hooper in right may have glittered more brightly offensively in other years, but in 1912 they did nothing to diminish their reputation as one of the best defensive outfields ever. "I used to sit up in my mezzanine box at Yankee Stadium years later and look at a pretty good outfield, too—Bob Meusel, Earle Coombs, and Babe Ruth," recalled former Yankees general manager Ed Barrow. "They were great, to be sure. But defensively I would rate Speaker, Lewis, and Hooper over them."

The Babe himself agreed. "Tris Speaker was right at the top of his game when I broke in [two years later], and Tris at his best came mighty near being the daddy of all fly chasers. But I think there's one man in my experience who was even better than Speaker. He comes as near being the perfect outfielder as any man I ever saw. This was Harry Hooper. He would take one squint, then turn his back and run to the place where the ball was headed. And in all his career I don't believe he misjudged a half dozen balls."

Lewis in left was another gem. He could negotiate the sharp incline in front of Fenway's left field wall so flawlessly that the hill became known as "Duffy's Cliff."

And the Golden Outfield could hit.

"Nuff Ced" and his heroes. Left to right: catcher Bill ("Rough") Carrigan, pitcher Fred Anderson, infielder Clyde Engle, McGreevey, manager Jake Stahl, and reliever Charley ("Sea Lion") Hall.

In 1911, each of the three had topped .300 (Lewis .307, Hooper .311, and Speaker .327). In 1912, Hooper fell drastically to .242, but Lewis hit a respectable .284, and superstar Speaker soared to .383, banging out 222 hits and, in spite of "Smoky Joe" Wood's 34 wins, won the Chalmers automobile as the league's most valuable player.

The late sportswriter Harry Grayson once wrote: "It's the only outfield that's discussed as a combination," and Boston fans contend that if the Hall of Fame has room for the great double-play team of Tinker, Evers, and Chance as a unit, then surely this trio should be reunited there. (Lewis has not yet been selected; Speaker and Hooper have both been individually.)

This then was the team that romped to the American League pennant, finishing 14 games ahead of Washington and 15 ahead of the favored Athletics. Because the pennant race was a runaway, the highlights of the regular season were two individual feats: the magnificent pitching streaks of the Senators' Walter ("Big Train") Johnson and the Red Sox' Wood, each of whom won 16 games in a row.

Earl Hamilton of the Browns ended Johnson's streak in the middle of August, at which time Wood had won 9 straight. His closest call had been a 1-0 squeaker over Ed Willet of Detroit. (These were the Tigers of Ty Cobb and Wahoo Sam Crawford, not an easy team to shut out.) By early September, Wood's skein had reached 13 and Washington was due at Fenway. Senators manager Clark Griffith telephoned Stahl and pleaded, "Why don't you let Walter defend his record. Let him work against Wood." And then, in an appeal to Stahl's counting-house instinct, Griffith added, "It'll mean a full house."

Wood remembers the occasion vividly. "The newspapers built it up like a prizefight. They gave our weights, biceps, and so on. The idea was to play up the champion versus challenger to build up the house." The promo surely worked. Fans overflowed the grandstand onto the fringes of the outfield, part of which had to be roped off for them. Thus the stage was set, in a somewhat cluttered fashion, for one of the finest pitching duels in Red Sox history.

One run decided it. In the sixth inning of a scoreless tie, Speaker hit a ground rule double into the crowd. Then Duffy Lewis lofted a fly ball down the right field line. Senators outfielder Danny Moeller dashed over madly but couldn't quite reach it, and Speaker scored the only run of the ball game. It was reported that in the locker room after the game, Johnson approached a tearful Moeller and offered this consolation: "Don't feel badly. I should have struck him out."

Wood went on to tie Johnson's record, strangely enough against the very man who had stopped Walter, Earl Hamilton of St. Louis. Wood beat him 2-1, Joe's sixteenth consecutive win, but the Tigers ended Joe's streak a few days later, on September 20. By this time the Sox had won the pennant, and the baseball world anxiously awaited their confrontation with the red-hot New York Giants, who had won the National League by 10 games and, not to be outdone, had in Rube Marquard a pitcher who had won 19 straight games, still the major league record today.

The World Series

Carrigan, Carrigan,
  Speaker, Lewis, Wood, and Stahl,
Bradley, Engle, Pape, and Hall,
  Wagner, Gardner, Hooper, too;
Hit them! Hit them! Hit them! Hit them!
Do boys, do.

—sung to the tune of "Tammany"
by the Royal Rooters
as they marched around Times Square
on the eve of the first game
of the 1912 World Series

This was the World Series the Giants fumbled away. Two superb ball teams played 74 innings, and when they were finished, they had determined that the difference between them was the Giants' miscues, without which the Red Sox could not have won. Because history demands that someone be assigned the blame, Fred Snodgrass has been made the scapegoat, though any of a number of other Giants contributed at least equally to the team's demise. Despite, or perhaps because errors decided this Series, it was fascinating and thrilling. There were wonderful fielding plays as well as dreadful ones,

star pitchers were bombed and long-shots delivered, loyal fans were snubbed and fair-weather friends provided for, and there were rhubarbs and a riot (or at least a stampede). And finally, this was a Series in which the team that won entered the final half-inning behind.

In 1912, the flip of a coin determined which team would host the first game of the World Series. John McGraw's Giants won the toss; thus on Tuesday, October 6, the first game was played at the Polo Grounds. For the next games the teams would alternate sites, but if a deciding game became necessary there would be another coin toss to determine its site.

Led by Mayor John ("Honey Fitz") Fitzgerald and the leader of the Boston Royal Rooters, Nuff Ced McGreevey, a thousand Bostonians and two brass bands filled four special trains for New York. This assortment of fanatics paraded up and down the field before the game, regaling the equally partisan New York fans with their renditions of "Tessie" and "When I Get You Alone

The Golden Outfield still looked trim when reunited in 1930. From left to right— as always—Lewis, Speaker, and Hooper.

53

Tonight." The unappreciative audience showered hoots and catcalls on the Bostonians.

"It will be Wood, of course, for the first game," announced Red Sox manager Stahl. Everyone expected McGraw to counter with the great veteran Christy Mathewson or the left-handed Rube Marquard, his "$11,000 Beauty." Instead, McGraw started his young rookie, Jeff Tesreau, who pitched well enough to win but was undone by his fielders. Outfielders Josh Devore and Fred Snodgrass allowed a fly ball to drop between them, and second baseman Larry Doyle muffed a double-play ball. The Red Sox parlayed the Giants' miscues and Wood's 11 strikeouts into a 4-3 victory. Led by the brass bands, the Royal Rooters proudly marched off to their train and had such an intoxicating good time on the trip home that for years afterward the New Haven Railroad referred to the journey as "the John Barleycorn Excursion."

At Fenway the next day, Honey Fitz presided over the ceremonies before the second game, presenting a new car to Jake Stahl and a silver bat with a red ribbon to Heinie Wagner. Armed with such good luck charms and the platitudinous praise of a publicity-seeking politician, the Sox survived against Mathewson thanks to five Giants errors. With the score tied 6-6 after the eleventh, umpire "Silk" O'Loughlin spared the Giants further embarrassment for the day when he bellowed, "Boys, it's just too dark to play." With a modicum of fielding support for Mathewson, the Giants would have won it, but they almost triumphed despite their errors. In the eleventh, Stahl brought in young Hughie Bedient, having already used Ray Collins and Sea

Lion Hall. The nervous rookie immediately hit Fred Snodgrass and walked Beals Becker, but smooth Rough Carrigan cut them both down stealing.

Discounting the tie as a home game for Boston, the teams stayed in Fenway, where in game three Bucky O'Brien lost a heartbreaking decision to Marquard after one of the most controversial plays in the Series. With one out in the bottom of the ninth and the Giants leading 2-0, Lewis beat out an infield tap and Larry Gardner stung a double to right, scoring Lewis. Jake Stahl hit sharply back to Marquard, who knocked down the ball and made a fine off-balance throw to third, nailing Gardner. Heinie Wagner then beat out a grounder, sending Jake to third, and stole second on the first pitch to Forrest Cady. With the winning runs now in scoring position, Cady drove a long fly to right field, where Josh Devore made a headlong leap for the ball. In the thick late afternoon mist that had gathered, it was only certain that Devore had picked himself up after the dive and run into the locker room as if he had caught the ball for the game's final out (though if he had missed he would have done the same thing). Half the fans left the park convinced that Devore had not caught the drive, and three different ones showed up the next day claiming that Devore couldn't have caught the ball because they had it. But the umpires ruled otherwise.

Tied 1-1 in games, the Series returned to New York. The hitting of Larry Gardner and the pitching of Joe Wood, who once again outdueled Jeff Tesreau, produced a 3-1 triumph. Gardner tripled, singled, and walked, and helped produce each of the Red Sox' runs.

The Sox took a 3-1 lead in games the next day at Fenway. Hughie Bedient allowed the Giants only

Opposite top: Walter ("Big Train") Johnson, only second best to Smoky Joe Wood in 1912. *Opposite bottom:* Babe Ruth's favorite "fly chaser," Harry Hooper. *Above:* the "Day of the Cossacks"—police rout Royal Rooters.

three hits; the Sox reached Mathewson for five, but all in the first three innings. Triples by Hooper and Yerkes and another error by Larry Doyle foiled Christy, whose patience with his fielders must have been wearing thin by this time.

"That was it," joyfully proclaimed the Boston papers. "Hugie's victory has sewed it up."

"I can use Wood tomorrow, and on Monday night we'll be back as the champs," an equally overconfident Stahl announced on Sunday to the crowd as he boarded the train for New York. Sunday baseball was not allowed in New York, so the players and the Royal Rooters had a day of leisure to contemplate what they felt sure was their impending success. But on Monday Red Sox owner McAleer turned their reveries into wishful thinking. "Jake, I think you should use O'Brien today," he advised.

"Oh, hell, Jimmy," Stahl replied, "Joe is all geared up for the game. I can't change now."

"You can and you will," commanded McAleer. "I'm still the president of this club. Give Wood another day of rest."

The last minute change must have upset O'Brien as much as Stahl. The pitcher yielded five runs to the Giants in the first before Stahl, still riled over McAleer's decision, brought in Collins. Ray threw seven shutout innings but in vain. Boston could do little against Marquard, and New York prevailed 5-2.

The train ride back to Boston threatened to be mutinous. "Why the hell doesn't McAleer run his end and let Jake run his," the troops groused.

Finally O'Brien had enough, both of the barbs and the bottle, and he

yelled, "For Christ's sake, I did the best I could!"

Joe Wood's brother Paul, who had lost a hundred dollars on the game, snarled, "Go to hell," and the fight was on. O'Brien arrived in Boston with a shiner as well as a lost ball game to his discredit.

It was a friendly tussle compared to the strife the next day, Tuesday, October 15, 1912, "the Day of the Cossacks." On this, one of the blackest days in Red Sox history, the Royal Rooters would end ten years of unswerving loyalty; some, it has even been whispered, would shift their allegiance to the Braves. The cause of their disenchantment was not the victory of the surging Giants, who scalded Smoky Joe for six runs in the first inning and an 11-4 win, but the seating mix-up that precipitated a near riot.

Apparently the management had oversold the park, and of all people, the Royal Rooters were the ones who lost their seats. With their bands defiantly blaring "Tessie" all over Fenway, the Rooters refused to leave the field until the management provided them with seats. But there were none to be provided, and finally, mounted police were called to herd the Rooters off the field. This show of force provoked a stampede. Cursing the Red Sox' management and, for good measure, John McGraw, the Rooters trampled the bleacher fence. One of the older Rooters, obviously many sheets to the wind, was seen standing on the broken fence, waving his derby and yelling, "To hell with Queen Victoria!"—apparently still a serviceable hate object, though she had been dead for many years and was not likely to have sinned against or heard of the Royal Rooters.

Clyde Engle. In 57 games in 1912 with the Red Sox, he played every infield position, but he is remembered for the famous soft fly ball he hit to Fred Snodgrass in the final game of the World Series.

The Red Sox had now lost two games and alienated their most loyal fans. To make matters worse, they had only the rookie Hugh Bedient to pitch in the seventh game against a well-rested Christy Mathewson. Bedient had beaten Mathewson in the fifth game but only with the generous assistance of the Giants' fielders. The bucket shops did not expect him to be as fortunate this time; even though the Red Sox won the coin toss and the game was to be played at Fenway, the bookies made the Giants 5-3 favorites.

The youthful Bedient yielded a run in the third on a walk to Josh Devore, two infield outs, and Red Murray's double. Otherwise he matched the flawless pitching of the immortal Matty until the sixth, when Larry Doyle smashed one toward the temporary right field bleachers. Harry Hooper raced back to the barrier, leaped to spear the ball, and disappeared among the crowd as he came down. The circus catch saved the game and the Series for Boston. Doyle later observed, "I never hit one better; I still think Hooper was off the playing field when he caught it." This time the umpires agreed with Boston.

Matty needed no such fielding gems. He would have been more than content had his fielders merely done what they were supposed to do. But in the seventh they sabotaged him again. With one out Jake Stahl lifted a short fly to left. Each of three players—Josh Devore, Art Fletcher, and Fred Snodgrass— probably could have caught it, but each deferred to another and the inevitable happened; Stahl ended up at second. Matty then walked Heinie Wagner to pitch to Bedient, so Stahl called for pinch hitter Olaf Henriksen, a 5-foot 7-inch, 155-pound

Dane whom the fans called "Swede." In this, his first and only time up in the Series, "Little Ollie" punched a two-strike double down the third base line, and the game was tied 1-1. Hooper then had a chance to put the Sox ahead, but he flied out to Snodgrass.

Joe Wood came in to pitch the last innings for Boston. Although he had been blasted the day before, Stahl's faith in him was unshaken. For two innings Wood held the Giants scoreless and the manager's judgment appeared sound. Unfortunately, Mathewson checked the Red Sox, and thus at the end of nine, the score remained tied.

In the tenth the Giants reached Wood for a run. With one out Red Murray doubled into the left field corner, and Fred Merkle followed with a scorching line drive to center that went for a double when Tris Speaker failed in his attempted shoestring catch on the ball. Wood eased a desperate situation by fanning Buck Herzog. Then he ended the inning by knocking down the drive of Chief Myers with his pitching hand and throwing the Indian out. Only one run had scored, but the damage to the Red Sox seemed fatal. Even if they could manage to tie the game in the bottom of the tenth, they would need a replacement for Wood, whose hand had already begun to swell. So instead of tying the game, they won it.

"We were more angry than nervous," Larry Gardner reminisced. "We knew what we had to do and set out to do it." Luckily they had help.

The lead-off hitter should have been Wood, normally a strong hitting pitcher. But having been incapacitated by Myers' line drive, Wood deferred to pinch hitter Clyde Engle,

The goat. It has been all but forgotten that with a fine running catch Snodgrass nearly saved the game he is charged with having muffed away.

who lifted a soft fly to Fred Snodgrass. For decades after, Fred would wail the same dirge: "I don't know why; I just dropped it." Indeed he did. Engle reached second, and the unnerved Matty grooved one to Harry Hooper. The right fielder hit it on the screws, but this time Snodgrass made a dashing, diving catch. And Engle, who had reached third, had to scamper back to second to avoid being doubled off. Can posterity be so unfair as to remember only Snodgrass' muff and not his great catch? Yes, and more so, for after Mathewson walked the next batter, Steve Yerkes, he faced Tris Speaker in a classic and crucial confrontation, the resolution of which should surely have absolved Snodgrass. With the tying run on third and the winning run on first, Matty fooled Speaker, and the Cowboy lifted a foul pop between first baseman Fred Merkle and catcher Chief Myers. The infielders surrounded it as ineffectually as Snodgrass, Fletcher, and Devore had surrounded the pop-up in the seventh, and the ball fell harmlessly to the turf. Most baseball writers divide the blame between Merkle and Myers, tactfully neglecting to mention that Matty himself could have caught the ball.

Giving a second life to Speaker at the plate was threatening one's own, as the Giants soon learned when Tris singled to right, scoring Engle with the tying run and sending Yerkes to third. There was still only one out. The game that Matty could already have won was tied and the winning run was on third. Duffy Lewis was walked to set up a force at the plate. Then third baseman Larry Gardner drove a fly ball to Josh Devore in deep right, and after the catch, Yerkes waltzed home with the Series winner. Gardner can't remember what kind of pitch he hit, but he will never forget the sights and sensations of that glorious victory: "I remember how the fans went wild and so did the players. We made about four thousand dollars each out of the Series; that kind of money went a long, long way back then."

History has done little to rectify the misconception about that turbulent ending. Both Fred Snodgrass and Chief Myers recently died. In Fred's obituary his misplay in the Series was prominently described and was alleged to have cost the Giants $30,000 as a team. In Myers' obituary there was no mention of the foul pop that dropped between him and Merkle. And Merkle? He has been saddled with a boner all his own—costing the Giants the pennant in 1908 by failing to run from first to second as the would-be winning run came home in the bottom of the ninth.

59

1915 and 1916

By 1915, manager Bill Carrigan had pretty much fashioned the team he wanted—excellent on the mound, strong on defense, and powerful enough at the plate to ensure victory. For pitchers he had his Mutt and Jeff combination—the 5-foot 7-inch Rube Foster and the 6-foot 4-inch Tar Heel, Ernie Shore, both of whom would enjoy their finest year in the majors—and two left handers, Babe Ruth and Dutch Leonard. In 1914, Leonard had turned in a record of 18-5 with the unbelievable ERA of 1.01. Backing up these four was the Hercules of 1912, Joe Wood. Smoky had suffered from arm trouble since 1912, but in 1915 he bounced back with one last fling as a starting pitcher, posting a highly creditable 15-5 record and leading the American League with an ERA of 1.49. The pitching staff was so incredibly strong that Carrigan could afford to keep the submarining rookie, Carl Mays, in the bullpen. As a reliever, Mays posted still another miniscule ERA, 1.54.

As great as the pitching was, it was immensely aided by an uncommonly strong defensive infield. Two West Virginians, Del Gainor and Dick Hoblitzel divided the first base duties; the veterans Jack Barry and Heinie Wagner shared second; Deacon Scott was at short; and the ever dependable Larry Gardner handled third.

It was in the outer garden, however, where the Red Sox really excelled. The Golden Outfield of Duffy Lewis, Tris Speaker, and Harry Hooper was second to none in baseball. If there were any doubters, they were surely hushed by the unit's play in the 1915 World Series.

Carrigan played some behind the plate, but he depended mainly on Hick Cady and Pinch Thomas. Both had been picked and trained by Bill, and he watched over them like a mother hen.

The pennant race was a tight one, but every time Hughie Jennings brought his Tigers close, the Red Sox would reassert themselves. "We won in 1915 over a tough Tiger team for the simple reason we could always beat them," chirps Larry Gardner. The facts support him. The Red Sox were 12-8 against Detroit; if the figures had been reversed, the Tigers, not the Red Sox, would have played the Phillies in the Series.

The Series itself was quite similar to the one between Oakland and Los Angeles in 1974. It went only five games but each game was a cliffhanger. "We've got to win this thing early," manager Bill Carrigan informed his charges in a pre-Series clubhouse meeting, "or we'll have to face [the Phillies' great Grover Cleveland ("Pete")] Alexander three times. We can probably count on a good game from Pete each time he works." Rough was right. The Red Sox faced Alexander only twice and he was tough both times. The first time was the opening game at Philadelphia, when he beat Ernie Shore 3-1, though Shore gave up a total of only five hits. The Phillies scored their winning two runs in the eighth without hitting a ball out of the infield. There was no way of knowing it at the time, but Ernie would be ill served by posterity for his efforts that day; he pitched a great game yet would be remembered as the only pitcher in history to lose a World Series game to the Phillies.

Game two started the march of three straight Red Sox victories by the same score, 2-1. On the mound

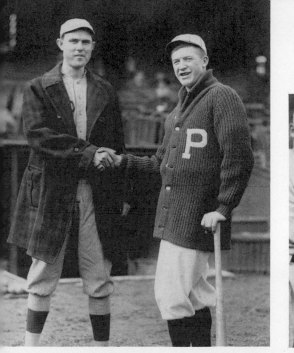

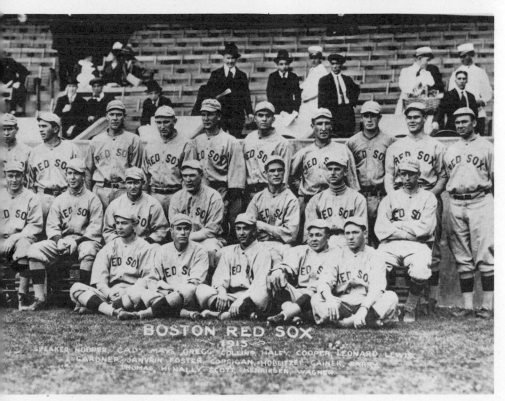

BOSTON RED SOX
1915
SPEAKER HOOPER CADY MAYS GREGG COLLINS HALEY COOPER LEONARD LEWIS
J. GARDNER JANVRIN FOSTER CORRIGAN HOBLITZEL GAINER BARRY
THOMAS McNALLY SCOTT HENRIKSEN WAGNER

Top left: Before first game of 1915 World Series, Ernie Shore, left, greets his mound opponent, Pete Alexander. *Top right:* Tris Speaker, right, meets his opposite number, Gavvy Cravath. *Above:* the champs.

61

Foster surrendered only three hits and at the plate he regained them. With one of his three hits, he drove in Larry Gardner with the winning run in the ninth.

Among those applauding Foster's mighty effort were Woodrow Wilson and his lady friend, Mrs. Edith Galt. It was the first time a President appeared at a World Series.

For the next two games the teams moved up the coast to Boston, where owner Joe Lannin took a tremendous gamble: in order to increase attendance, he arranged to play the games at brand new Braves Field. It paid off handsomely. Not only did he gain a larger crowd (42,300, a World Series record at the time) but he made possible a remarkable, game-saving catch by Duffy Lewis. It came in the third inning on Gavvy Cravath's 400-foot drive, which would have easily been over the left field

wall at Fenway. In the meantime Dutch Leonard hurled a second three-hitter at the Phillies. The Red Sox made six hits off Alexander, three of them by fielding hero Duffy Lewis, and the American Leaguers won their second 2-1 game.

Game four turned out to be a repeat of the day before. Ernie Shore got his second chance, and this time he held the Phillies to just one run. Once again Lewis knocked in the winning run in a 2-1 game, and once again he made a tremendous catch on Cravath. For the rest of his life Gavvy would lament, "Why, oh why, didn't we play those games at Fenway?"

The fifth and final game, in Philadelphia, showed once and for all that destiny just wasn't on the side of Philadelphia. Philly owner Bill Baker also wanted more fans at the game, so he installed temporary bleachers

Above: Harry Hooper slides safely into third in Series' second game. *Opposite:* Hooper cracks Series-winning homer in fifth game off Phillies' Eppa Rixey.

in center field, shortening the distance between the stands and home plate. Harry Hooper hit two home runs into the extra seats, equaling his output for 149 games in the regular season. "I put those seats in so more of our fans could see those games," Baker pleaded in defense afterward.

"You did it to get more money," replied the Philadelphia papers, "you Midas, you."

Hooper's home runs were the margin of victory, and the Red Sox ended it all 5-4. For the third time Boston had won a World Series. The Red Sox had won on superb pitching (all Boston starters had gone the distance—Shore twice, Foster twice, and Leonard once) and outstanding play by the Golden Outfield. Lewis led the regulars with a .444 Series average; Hooper hit .350 and Speaker .294. They made 20 of the

Sox' 38 hits in the Series and knocked in eight of the team's twelve runs. Boston had three home runs, two by Hooper and one by Lewis. Ty Cobb, attending the Series as a reporter, stated, "The Red Sox' outfield play was the best I've seen in many a year."

Tim Murnane of the Boston *Globe* picked out Lewis for special accolades. "Duffy Lewis was the real hero of this Series, or any other," he wrote. "I have witnessed all of the contests for the game's highest honors in the last 30 years and I want to say that the all-around work of the modest Californian never has been equalled in a big Series."

Until the opening day of the season, the 1915 world champions were picked to defend their title successfully in 1916. Then the Boston *Globe* headlines announced a potential disaster: "Tris Speaker sold to Cleveland for $50,000 and two obscure players." Lannin had had a spat with the center fielder and had felt compelled to assert his authority. However ill-conceived his decision to sell Speaker, he compensated somewhat for it when he purchased Tilly Walker, a solid hitter, from St. Louis for center field. The whole deal was very complicated (Speaker later received part of the purchase price), and once again the mysterious hand of American League President Ban Johnson was involved. Ban wanted to help Cleveland develop a winning team.

With Speaker gone manager Carrigan had to depend even more on his pitchers. Led by Babe Ruth and Carl Mays and assisted by the three heroes of 1915, Ernie Shore, Dutch Leonard, and Rube Foster, the Sox finished on top, two games ahead of the second place White Sox.

It looked for a while as if their World Series rivals would once again be the Phillies, but when the National League race was over Uncle Wilbert Robinson had Brooklyn on top. Robinson had learned his baseball as a lad in Hudson, Massachusetts, while working in his father's butcher shop. One of the Royal Rooters (never truly the same after 1912 but still running around and singing "Tessie") hoisted a sign proclaiming, "We'll cut up Robbie just like one of his old man's ribs of beef." And though Brooklyn threw a scare into the Sox, that is just about what Boston did.

This time the Series was due to start in Boston. Once again Lannin decided to use Braves Field, and once again Carrigan opened with Ernie Shore. "When I have a real important game," Carrigan told the press, "I'd rather have Ernie out there than anyone."

Robby tried southpaw Rube Marquard. His scouting reports were explicit: "The Red Sox can't hit left handers." It wasn't quite true, but it was Brooklyn's sloppy fielding not Red Sox power that decided the game. The Dodgers' shortstop, Ivy Olson, had a particularly bad time. Ivy had spent several years in the American League, and most of the Red Sox remembered him well. Their chant became, "When in doubt, hit to Olson."

By the ninth the Sox were leading 6-1 with Shore working smoothly. Then Brooklyn scored three runs (included in the rally was a single by Casey Stengel—yes, he once was young), knocking out Shore. In came Carl Mays. He was greeted with an infield single by Hi Myers, making the score 6-5, and the bases were still loaded. It took a great stop on Bill Daubert by Deacon Scott to save

64

Top: Brooklyn manager Uncle Wilbert
Robinson, third from left, and Boston
skipper Carrigan, second from right, meet
umpires before start of 1916 Series game.
Bottom: Carrigan and owner Joe Lannin
flank Lannin's son, Paul, at Series

the game. The Red Sox had won the opener, but barely.

The next game was one of the greatest pitching duels in baseball history. Brooklyn scored in the first when Hi Myers hit a line drive that bounced over center fielder Tilly Walker's head. Before Walker could return the ball to the plate, Myers had an inside-the-park home run. Boston tied it in the third on a triple by Deacon Scott and a ground out. And that's how it stood until Brooklyn starter Sherry Smith weakened a bit in the fourteenth. Dick Hoblitzel walked and was sacrificed to second by Duffy Lewis. Carrigan sent in Mike McNally to run for Hoblitzel and right-handed-hitting Del Gainor to hit for port-sider Larry Gardner. Gainor doubled to left, scoring McNally with the winner.

The Red Sox pitcher, who had also gone all the way, walked over to manager Carrigan exulting, "I told you I could handle those goddamn National Leaguers."

"You sure did," replied Bill, "they don't see many pitchers like you in their league." The pitcher was Babe Ruth. None of his home runs gave him more joy than that 14-inning win against Brooklyn.

The teams now moved down to the borough of churches, where Robby came up with Connie Mack's old hero, Jack Coombs, and Carrigan chose Carl Mays. Neither of them lasted to the finish, at which Brooklyn emerged victorious 4-3. It was the Dodgers' only spark in the Series. Dutch Leonard won the fourth game 6-2 (Larry Gardner's three-run homer was the key), and Ernie Shore three-hit the Dodgers back in Boston, beating them 4-1 and ending the Series by the same count.

The Red Sox had now won two World Series in a row, the only time

66

Top: Red Sox' Tilly Walker triples against Dodgers in first inning of first game. *Above:* Hooper leads off. *Right:* Dutch Leonard.

they have done so in their history. They reigned the baseball world, but not for long. In the next three years there were to be changes in the Red Sox and in baseball in general. First, Carrigan quit and went back to Maine. Then Joe Lannin sold the club to Harry Frazee (like Lannin a former bellhop). New England was to learn there were some bellhops and then again there were other bellhops.

Frazee's Sox finished second in 1917 and won a wartime championship in 1918. In 1919, the hard-throwing left hander who had won the thriller from Sherry Smith three years before started to hit home runs at an astonishing clip. Bill Carrigan's pitching and defense game was about to undergo revolutionary changes. They could have made Fenway the capital of the new game, but Harry Frazee had other plans.

Opposite top: Carrigan at bat against Brooklyn. *Above:* the irrepressible Royal Rooters in Brooklyn.

1946

From 1934 to 1946, Tom Yawkey spent hundreds of thousands of dollars, maybe more than a million, trying to acquire a great team. Eventually he did. Indeed, the Red Sox teams of 1938 through 1942 were fine ones, but unfortunately Boston happened to be in the same league as the New York Yankees—at least technically. It was at this time that it used to be said, "The Red Sox will win in the American League, and the Yankees will win in their league." In all but 1940, when the Tigers captured the flag by one game, this prediction held true. In 1941, the Red Sox finished in second place, 7 games ahead of the third-place White Sox, but 17 games behind Joe McCarthy's Yankees. In 1942, they finished 10½ games ahead of the third-place St. Louis Browns, but 9 behind the Yankees. The prewar Sox outclassed and were outclassed.

A similar fate had befallen the 1928 Athletics, who finished second to the Yankees but far from third. Yet with essentially the same team, Connie Mack's Athletics murdered the rest of the league in 1929, 1930, and 1931, and are today considered to have been one of the truly great teams of all time. So too would the Red Sox, with no change in key personnel, transform themselves from champion runners-up to champions.

Because its nucleus was the same as the 1942 team's, the great Red Sox team in 1946 came as a surprise to Sox fans. Four starters from 1942—Ted Williams, Johnny Pesky, Dominic DiMaggio, and Bobby Doerr —were the heart of the Red Sox, not only in 1946 but (excluding the war years of 1943-45) from 1942 until

1952, when Ted would leave for Korea, Doerr would retire, and Pesky would be traded to Detroit.

What made champions of the 1946 Red Sox? First, the slump of the New York Yankees. The Bombers of 1946 were inferior to those of 1942. Joe DiMaggio, Charlie Keller, and Tommy Henrich all skidded, and Joe Gordon went from .322 to .210. On the other hand, the Red Sox' pitching improved dramatically, particularly after the addition of Dave ("Boo") Ferriss. Both Joe Dobson and Tex Hughson had similar years in 1942 and in the pennant-winning year of 1946, but Ferriss' 1946 performance was an unexpected bonus. He had won 21 games in 1945, but that was a year when lineups were still crippled by the war. The three

Yankees bat against Red Sox at Yankee Stadium, August 11, 1946. By this time Boston had all but clinched the pennant.

leading hitters in the American League that year were Snuffy Stirnweiss (.309), 38-year-old Tony Cuccinello (.308), and Johnny Dickson (.302). In 1946, Boo was pitching against the top talent, and he did it uncommonly well.

Ferriss began his great season by winning his first 10 games, dropping a few, then winning 12 more. During the entire season he never lost at Fenway Park, and in the World Series there he shut out the Cardinals on six hits. He finished the regular season with a record of 25-6, probably the best a Red Sox pitcher had done since Joe Wood won 34 and lost 5 in 1912.

Ferriss could not only pitch but field his position superbly and even hit respectably (a .250 lifetime bat-

ting average). And he could get along with everyone, not a common trait in a star. Johnny Pesky, a man not prone to flattery, once exclaimed, "What a guy! He's the only man I ever knew in baseball who never had an unkind word to say."

A touch of the bizarre to seal the legend: Joe Dobson has verified the persistent rumor that Ferriss was completely ambidextrous. Dobson says, "Those reports about Dave being able to throw with both hands weren't baloney; when his right arm went bad, several of us asked him to try with his left arm, but he wouldn't do it." In 1946, his right arm was good enough for a league-leading winning percentage of .806, the crucial ingredient in the Sox' winning recipe.

Hughson's record in 1946 was 20-11. With sheaves of statistics to support their contention, many New England fans claim that in 1946 Hughson was a more complete pitcher than Ferriss was. Ferriss himself was quoted as saying, "Whenever I pitch, they seem to get me a lot of runs in the beginning; they don't do the same for Tex." Regardless of who was the better pitcher that year, Hughson and Ferriss gave Boston its greatest one-two punch since the teens.

Joe Dobson (13-6) and likable southpaw Mickey Harris (17-9) completed the big four. It was just another strong year for the dependable Dobson, but for Mickey it was his best. (It included a highly creditable winning streak of seven games.)

The bullpen staff was led by Bob Klinger (acquired in May), Ernie Johnson, Mace Brown, and that wonderful old campaigner, Mike Ryba, a versatile sort whose skills included championship-caliber hotel-lobby sitting. In one particularly happy month of lobby sitting, he counted 35 weddings. Despite the diverse talents of Ryba, the bullpen wasn't the best in the league. This Red Sox team really didn't need a great one.

When manager Joe Cronin looked over his roster in early 1946, he saw five set positions and three question marks. His catchers, Hal Wagner and Roy Partee, were not outstanding but adequate. Doerr was set at second, Pesky at short, Williams in left, and DiMaggio in center. Cronin needed help at first base, so he sent Eddie Lake to Detroit for Rudy York—one of the best trades Boston ever made. "The Big Indian" knocked in 119 runs, second on the team to Williams (123) and third in the league to Williams and

Hank Greenberg of Detroit (127). (Bobby Doerr was fourth with 116.)

Third base was a more difficult problem. Ernie Andres was the first choice there and covered the position well but he hit poorly. During the season the Sox used no less than seven players at third. The bulk of the work went to Rip Russell and Mike ("Pinky") Higgins, who had returned to Boston from Detroit in May. Before the opening of the World Series, Cronin told the newspapers, "This is what we've been saving Higgins for; he's our third baseman." Pinky played all seven games at third in the Series.

Right field was patrolled mostly by two journeymen, left-handed hitting George ("Catfish") Metkovich and right-handed Tom McBride. Another outfielder, and the closest player on the team to a supersub, was Leon Culberson, who played in 59 games and hit .313.

This was basically the team Boston presented on opening day in the nation's capital in April 1946. After Harry Truman had thrown out the first ball, Hughson throttled the Senators, Williams blasted a home run, and Boston prevailed 6-3. It was an impressive opening by a strong team, but the Yankees were considered invincible. Most experts picked Boston to finish either second or third, depending on how well the Tigers did. The faithful from Bangor to New Haven talked pennant, but a quick review of recent history soon convinced many of them that they were deluding themselves. They shouldn't have been so cynical. As matters turned out, there was no pennant race. The Sox won the season series from the two favorites, New York and Detroit, 14-8 and 15-7, respectively, and finished 12 games ahead of the Tigers and 17 ahead of the supposedly unbeatable Yanks.

In the Sox' first game with New York, on April 25, true to form the Yanks won 12-5, knocking out Hughson. The fans shook their heads and muttered, "Same old story; it's great until we play New York." Then a strange thing happened. Like the persistent General Grant continuing to attack after his army had been mauled in the Battle of the Wilderness, the Red Sox beat the Yankees by the same score the very next day. Boston then won 15 straight games through May 10, and the Red Sox fans began to sense that this year was going to be different. By the All-Star break, the Sox were far ahead of the field at 54-23, and New England wondered not whether but when this team would clinch the flag. In the meantime the fans diverted themselves by arguing over Ted Williams' reaction to the defense that manager Lou Boudreau of Cleveland had devised for him. "The Boudreau Shift" (later to be adopted by Eddie Dyer of the Cardinals in the World Series) placed four infielders on the right side of the infield for the pull-hitting slugger. Instead of hitting to the left side to beat the shift, as Ty Cobb advised, Williams stuck to his power pull hitting. His batting average dropped from .356 in 1942 to .342 in 1946, but his home run production increased slightly (from 36 to 38).

For those less inclined to debate, there was the pleasant diversion of speculating whether this team would eclipse the Sox' all-time win record of 105, set in 1912.

The Sox' success brought huge numbers of New Englanders to the

Celebrating a 14-9 pasting of Chicago, Boston's thirteenth win in a row through May 8, are, left to right, Dom DiMaggio, Rudy York, Johnny Pesky, and Ted Williams.

73

ball park, passing the old attendance mark of 730,340, set in 1942. By the end of the year, 1,416,944 fans had paid their way into Fenway. The Red Sox rewarded most of them, playing 60-17 ball at home. Public relations director Ed Doherty was quoted as saying, "Hell, we had to go over to Kenmore Square telling people we had no more seats." The 22 games the Sox played with the Yankees in New York and Boston drew more than 600,000.

Several writers have harped on the Sox' six-game losing streak in September, but when the Sox finally did clinch the pennant on September 13 (on a great game by Hughson and the only inside-the-park home run of Williams' career), their lead over the field was still a substantial 14 games. The team never did equal the record of Jake Stahl's 1912 team, falling short by 1 game, and it may not have been Yawkey's greatest team (the 1949 squad was no worse), but it surely gave New England fans something that only the most ancient could remember— a laugher of a pennant race.

The World Series

After the ease with which they had romped through the 1946 season, the Sox waited impatiently for the National League race to end. Johnny Pesky declared, "It was like a kid waiting for the last week or two of school to get out in the summer." Then, when the regular season ended, the pennant race still hadn't; the Dodgers and Cardinals finished in a tie for first, necessitating a three-game playoff to resolve the deadlock.

Hoping to keep his team from going stale and realizing it would be facing one of two red-hot teams, Cronin arranged a series of three games between Boston and an array of American League players. In the first game (on October 1, a very raw day), journeyman pitcher Mickey Haefner may have cost the Red Sox the 1946 World Series. He threw an inside curve to Ted Williams that struck the slugger squarely on the elbow and sent him in excruciating pain to the hospital for X rays. They proved negative, but the elbow had swollen to three times its normal size. The swelling had been reduced by the time the Series started, but the elbow was not back to normal until long after the Cardinals were the world champions. Ted doesn't alibi—it's not his nature—but the injury must have affected his efforts at the plate against St. Louis. He hit a dismal .200 (5 singles in 25 at-bats) and, it must be said, failed the Sox in the clutch.

Despite the injury to Williams, the Sox looked like sure winners before and even after the Series began. Boston had never lost a fall classic before 1946, and the Sox were heavily favored (20-7) to win this one. Bruised elbow or not, Williams would be aiming at a 310-foot fence down the right field line in St. Louis —thought to be an inviting target for the man who had strafed some of the National League's best pitchers in the All-Star Game, played at Fenway that year. Williams had banged out four hits, including two homers, and knocked in five runs in the junior circuit's 12-0 thrashing of the National League. (One of his homers had come off Rip Sewell's baffling blooper pitch, or "eephus ball.") Especially after the All-Star Game, the American League was considered to be far superior to the National League, and the experts noted with some awe that the Red Sox had just devastated the junior circuit.

The Series started at Sportsman's Park on October 6 with the Sox' Tex Hughson facing 21-game winner Howie Pollet. It was no Boston runaway, but with the help of a bad-bounce hit in the ninth that tied the score, the Sox won 3-2 in 10. Hughson and Ernie Johnson held St. Louis to seven hits. The big blow was Rudy York's tenth-inning clout into a refreshment stand atop the left field bleachers.

St. Louis took the second game behind the four-hit shutout pitching of Harry ("the Cat") Brecheen, who was particularly effective against Williams; Ted failed to hit the ball out of the infield. The teams now

took a day off to journey back to Boston. "We'll handle this thing back at Fenway," remarked Joe Cronin. "The boys are not going to want to come back to St. Louis."

The third game seemed to justify his cockiness. "I had everything breaking right," said Boo Ferriss after he shut out the Cardinals 4-0. York banged one into the screen with two on in the very first inning, deciding the game at the outset. Williams still wasn't hitting, but for the moment he didn't have to. To the fans' delight, the slugger beat out a bunt in the third inning.

In the fourth game St. Louis once and for all abrogated any thought of an easy Series. After the game, Redbirds manager Eddie Dyer jubilantly yelled, "That wipes out the

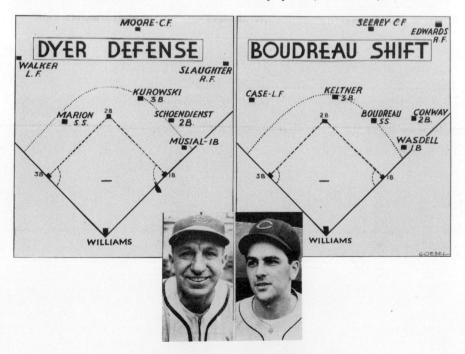

Two of the radical defenses against Ted Williams, and their architects—
Cards manager Eddie Dyer, left, and Indians chief, Lou Boudreau.

sting of that twelve-nothing All-Star beating!" His Cardinals had just drowned the Red Sox 12-3 in a flood of 20 base hits. Enos ("Country") Slaughter, Whitey Kurowski, and Joe Garagiola (a better ball player than he acknowledges on television) produced four hits each against the six pitchers Cronin called on in a vain attempt to stop the onslaught.

"I've got Dobson for them today," crowed the irrepressible Cronin the next morning. "He'll cool off their bats." He did. If not for two errors by Pesky, he probably would have had a shutout, but the Bosox' 11-hit attack sufficed in a 6-3 win.

For the third time the Red Sox led in the Series, and this time they were only one win from the world championship. They returned to St. Louis with Mickey Harris and Boo Ferriss rested and presumably ready for the Cardinals. But the Cards were ready too. A three-run third inning, which knocked out Harris, and another of Brecheen's great pitching performances led St. Louis to a 4-3 victory in the sixth game, despite Tex Hughson's strong relief effort. The Series was tied again, and Williams still wasn't hitting. "I'm sure due to hit one," noted Ted with considerable understatement. Yet Cronin remained serene. His ace, Boo Ferriss, was well rested and very eager for his second start of the Series against the little right hander, Murray Dickson, whom he and the Sox had beaten in the second game. Each team sent the rest of its staff to the bullpen. Brecheen said, "We'll have all winter to rest."

In the finale Boston began as if it had already allowed the Series to last too long. Wally Moses, a 36-year-old veteran who must have sensed that this would be his only

Series (he went 5 for 12), led off with a sharp single through the middle, and Pesky followed with another in practically the same place, sending Moses to third. Dominic's long fly to right scored Moses easily after the catch and brought up Williams. He lifted a towering smash to deep center—too far to left fielder Harry Walker's left but not out of the range of center fielder Terry Moore, though he was playing Williams considerably to the right of straightaway center. Off with the crack of the bat, Moore made an outstanding running catch on Ted and thereby probably saved Dickson and possibly all the Cardinals. The odds are very good that had Moore not caught Ted's drive, Dyer would have yanked Dickson immediately, but with Moore's grab (and some additional fielding gems later), Dickson would last seven long innings before the Bosox dispatched him. Now, he retired York on a pop-up, ending the first, and a promising threat had yielded only one run.

St. Louis threatened in the bottom of the inning, but Ted threw out Red Schoendienst trying to stretch a single. As the Cards' Stan Musial later doubled, Williams' throw undoubtedly saved a run. In the second inning Doerr reached third with one out but died there. This inning was the Cardinals' turn to score. Whitey Kurowski doubled, moved to third as Garagiola grounded out behind the runner, and scored on Walker's line drive to Williams.

Walker's great catch on another Williams shot and Moore's second spectacular grab—this one on Pinky Higgins—kept the score tied at 1-1 until the fifth, when the Cardinals knocked out Ferriss. The crushing blow was a double by the very man the Sox might have been rid of four

Bobby Doerr greets Rudy York at the plate after York's game-winning homer in the tenth inning of first 1946 Series game.

innings earlier, pitcher Dickson. Only the superb relief work of Joe Dobson kept the damage to two runs.

Still trailing 3-1 in the eighth, Cronin started the maneuvering that almost won the game. First he used second-line third baseman Rip Russell to hit for catcher Hal Wagner, and the pinch hitter singled to center. Then Catfish Metkovich, hitting for Dobson, doubled to left, sending Russell to third. This flurry brought Dyer from the dugout and Brecheen from the bullpen. "I'd been saving Brecheen for just this," remarked Eddie. "I knew he'd only had one day's rest [the teams had rested for a day after the sixth game], but I figured I could still get two good innings from him." The Cat almost squirmed out of trouble. He fanned Moses and retired Pesky on a short liner to Slaughter, but Dom DiMaggio rammed a double to right center, tying the score. When DiMaggio twisted his ankle coming into second and was replaced by Lee Culberson, it seemed a harsh but reasonable price to pay for a tie game, but the Bosox would soon keenly regret the loss of their fleet center fielder. Still, with the lead run on second, the Red Sox had cause for hope with Williams at the plate. Facing Dickson he had twice been robbed by the Cardinals' outfield, but against Brecheen he could manage only a pop-up to Schoendienst. The spurt had fizzled.

Having hit for Dobson in the top of the eighth, Cronin now had to make a pitching change. His choice proved to be unfortunate—Bob Klinger—and thus a ripe target for second guessers. With the left-handed hitting Slaughter leading off, why not use the lefty Ernie Johnson, or if Cronin wanted a right hander, Tex Hughson? Although Klinger had pitched some great relief ball throughout the year, he had not thrown a ball during the Series. Now Cronin was using him for the most crucial situation of the year.

Country Slaughter greeted Klinger with a single to center. Trying to sacrifice, Whitey Kurowski popped to Klinger, and then Del Rice flew deep to Williams. With two outs and Slaughter still on first, Harry ("the Hat") Walker hit the line drive to center that Boston fans still replay in their nightmares. The outfield was swung to the right for Harry, so Culberson had to cover considerable ground before he retrieved the ball. Would DiMaggio have reached the ball sooner? Would he have thrown it all the way home instead of relaying it to Pesky? "It was a two-out situation; of course I was running all the way," said Slaughter later. Pesky took Culberson's relay in short center field and, according to newspaper accounts, paused for a momentous second. When he finally realized Slaughter was going home, his throw was hurried and off target. It arrived between three and ten feet up the baseline from the plate (it depends on whose account you credit), and Slaughter scored. Klinger departed in favor of Johnson, who retired the side without further scoring, but the Cardinals were ahead 4-3.

The Sox mounted a last effort in the ninth. York and Doerr both singled. Paul Campbell ran for York. Pinky Higgins bunted to third, and Kurowski threw to second, forcing Doerr. One out now, the tying run, Campbell, only 90 feet away, and the lead run, Higgins, on first. Roy Partee, who had replaced catcher Hal Wagner, fouled out to Musial. Tom McBride, batting for pitcher Ernie Johnson, was the Sox' last hope. On his ground ball to Schoen-

Victorious Cardinals, from left to right: Enos ("Country") Slaughter, Harry ("the Cat") Brecheen, manager Eddie Dyer, Harry ("the Hat") Walker.

diest, a gasp escaped the St. Louis crowd as the ball ran up the red-head's sleeve for a fascinating moment. But he recovered just in time to nail Higgins at second for a force.

These were before the days of champagne. In the Cardinals' locker room the victors were celebrating with beer and mayhem. Walker yelled, "I hit a low pitch that was sinking—a good pitch, a good pitch."

The Red Sox' locker room might have been Fall River, Massachusetts, in the middle of the Depression.

Ferriss was crushed. "I can't understand it. I had my stuff today. Those were good pitches they hit."

Finally chastened, Cronin gave credit to the Cardinals. "Slaughter, Moore, and Walker—there's no better outfield around," the dejected manager said. "It was those three catches—by Moore and Walker on Williams and by Moore on Higgins—that's what beat us."

Williams was incommunicado. It was later reported that he sobbed in the shower.

1949

Since the end of World War II, the Red Sox have four times won or lost the American League pennant in the dying days of the season. One of these years, the gloriously successful 1967, was the Impossible Dream come true; in the other three years the Sox have been left tilting at windmills. The near misses of 1948 and 1972 drained the adrenalin from Boston fans, but the debacle of 1949 virtually crushed their spirits. This more than any other was a pennant the Sox should have won and didn't, thanks to two season-ending losses to the Yankees that gave the flag to the hated New Yorkers. Maybe the Sox' fans have always despised the Yankees because New York was always winning, or maybe because they can never forget Harry Frazee, or maybe just because of the geographical proximity of the two teams. Whatever the cause, Sox fans see villains in pinstripes, and 1949 gave them more reason to than ever before.

After the close finish of 1948 (see pages 114-17), Boston fans looked toward the 1949 season with high hopes. These were ingloriously doused when the team started disastrously. By the end of May, the Sox were 12 games back.

Then they started to move. The team found a one-two combination to rival Ferriss and Hughson of the 1946 club. One was Mel Parnell, a 25-year-old left hander who would win more games that year (25) than any southpaw in Red Sox history. His partner, Ellis Kinder, was best described by one of his teammates: "Ellie could drink more bourbon and pitch more clutch baseball than anyone I ever knew." Kinder would win

23 games; his liquor consumption went unrecorded.

Powered by an MVP year from Ted Williams and Dom DiMaggio's 34-game hitting streak, the Sox were only a game and a half out on Labor Day.

First baseman Billy Goodman, at .298, second baseman Bobby Doerr, .309, shortstop Vern Stephens, .290 and 159 RBIs, and third baseman Johnny Pesky, .306, comprised one of the best hitting infields of all time —another major factor in the Sox' move into contention in September.

On the morning of September 24, after having held the league lead and relinquished it, Boston was two games off the pace. Both New York and Boston had eight games left, five against each other. Here is the way that season finished—a finish that broke New England's heart.

September 24

A crisp Indian summer afternoon at Fenway—the type of day that turns paradisal with a Red Sox win over the Yankees. Manager Joe McCarthy sent Ellis Kinder after his thirteenth win in a row and the Red Sox' eighth straight. Yankees skipper Casey Stengel countered with lefty Ed Lopat, but this day "Steady Eddie" was jolted.

Doerr opened the second with a single to right. Al Zarilla walked, and Billy Goodman turned an attempted sacrifice into a bunt single, loading the bases. Lopat fooled Birdie Tebbetts and he popped up for the first out. Then came the turning point. Kinder grounded to first baseman Tommy Henrich, who threw to the plate and nailed Doerr, but Yankees catcher Yogi Berra threw badly to first in trying for the double play. Henrich stopped the throw, but noth-

Once again, the pitching would need no more offensive support but Ted Williams provided it anyway with a tremendous two-run clout deep into the right field bleachers over the 380-foot sign. Boston won 4-1. The Red Sox and Yankees were tied for first.

September 26

In Yankee Stadium now, the teams did battle with their second-line hurlers, young Mickey McDermott for Boston against New York's Tommy Byrne. Neither would last to the finish. New York carried a 6-3 lead into the top of the eighth, when the Sox rallied against reliever Joe Page. Birdie Tebbetts singled and was replaced by runner Tommy O'Brien. Lou Stringer, batting for relief pitcher Jack Kramer, walked. Dom DiMaggio then lined a shot over shortstop Phil Rizzuto, who jumped as high as a 5-foot 6-inch man can but succeeded only in deflecting it. O'Brien scored and Stringer went to third. Pesky followed with a ground ball to second baseman Stirnweiss, but George couldn't handle it, and Stringer scored. The Red Sox trailed by only one run, 6-5.

With two men on base now and still no one out, Ted Williams slashed one between first and second. Henrich lunged for it and observed the rest of the play resting on his backside without the ball. However, Stirnweiss had positioned himself deep in the hole in short right for the powerful, pull-hitting Williams. Now he grabbed the grounder, only to find that Joe Page hadn't covered first. With the bases loaded, Vern Stephens' fly to right sent DiMaggio home and the ever-alert Pesky to third.

The score was tied with one out.

ing stopped Zarilla, who scored from second. Dom DiMaggio then singled home Goodman; the Sox led 2-0.

Ted Williams later homered (his first off Lopat), but Kinder needed no more help. He limited New York to six hits in a 4-1 triumph. The Sox were now only one game out.

September 25

Sunday and at Fenway another beautiful day that 35,717 fans fully appreciated when the Red Sox nearly duplicated Saturday's performance. This time Mel Parnell was pitted against Allie Reynolds as Boston sought its ninth straight. The fans wouldn't have believed it, but it was to be the last game of the year in Boston.

The Red Sox loaded the bases in the first but couldn't score. Their frustration ended next inning. Johnny Pesky singled with the bases loaded and Boston jumped ahead 2-0.

Now came the play of the game. Doerr bunted, trying to squeeze home Pesky. The play came to the plate. It was preciously close, but veteran umpire Bill Grieves spread his arms in the safe sign. Yankees catcher Ralph Houk erupted, Ole Case scurried out and vented his wrath, but all to no avail. Pesky was safe and the Red Sox were ahead 7-6. His was the last run of the game. McCarthy brought in Kinder for two strong innings of relief, and the Red Sox were in first place.

After the game, Yankee Cliff Mapes accosted Grieves. Mapes hadn't been in the game, but the thought of World Series money always means more to a .247 hitter. "How much did you bet on the game, you SOB?" he asked pointedly. His honesty (that is, his honor) challenged, the veteran umpire rushed at Mapes, but peacemakers intervened and a fistfight was narrowly averted. (Mapes was fined $200 and later apologized to Grieves.)

Cal Hubbard, another veteran umpire, commented sharply, "How can a team that walks a man, makes an error, and then fails to cover first on a play blame the umpire for losing? Horsemeat!"

September 27

Connie Mack brought his Athletics to Yankee Stadium and Boston moved to Washington. Boston's Bobby Doerr banged three hits and Joe Dobson pitched well enough to preserve a 6-4 victory. Ted Williams knocked in his one hundred fifty-ninth run of the year, his last of the season. Meanwhile, the Yankees kept pace, winning 3-1 on Vic Raschi's three-hitter against the Athletics.

September 28

The Return of Dracula—Ray Scarborough, who had spellbound the Sox in the heat of the 1948 pennant fight, did it again.

Boston started 20-year-old Chuck Stobbs, and for eight innings he was superb. With a 1-0 lead entering the last frame, McCarthy decided to play his aces. First he brought in Kinder—he pitched to only one man, Sam Dente, who singled. Then came Mel Parnell, but he too failed. Washington tied the game and pushed runners to second and third. Senators manager Joe Kuhel then sent up old pro Buddy Lewis with orders to bunt home the winner. Parnell read the play and pitched out. Left-handed hitting Lewis couldn't have reached the ball with a polo mallet, and the runner from third, Eddie Robinson, slid right into the tag. The runner on second scurried to third on the play. Unable to steal the winning run, the Senators had it gift wrapped and presented to them. Parnell unleashed a wild pitch and Washington won 2-1, a four-hit victory for Scarborough.

Back in New York, the Yankees beat the Athletics on home runs by Bobby Brown and Jim Delsing, whose next claim to fame would be as the member of the Browns who ran for Bill Veeck's midget. The game provided a reversal of roles for Allie Reynolds and reliever Joe Page when Reynolds came out of the bullpen to preserve Page's victory. Boston and New York were tied again.

September 30

Both teams were rained out on the twenty-ninth and decided to play their games on the open day they had on Friday, the thirtieth. This may have been the weirdest game of the year for the Red Sox. They beat Washington 11-9 on five hits and 14 walks. Walter ("Bat") Masterson got the win. This performance was less than artistic, but the victory hurt the Yankees just the same. Ferris Fain hit two home runs and Dick Fowler baffled New York completely as Philadelphia won 4-1. Boston had regained its one-game lead, with only two games to go.

October 1

A schedule maker's masterpiece: two games in mammoth Yankee Stadium on a Saturday and Sunday to decide the pennant winner—Reynolds and Raschi against Parnell and Kinder. As if the series opener needed any more commemoration, the New York management had designated it "Joe DiMaggio Day," and plied the great one with everything from an automobile to 300 quarts of ice cream.

Mrs. Rosalie DiMaggio had been flown in from the West Coast for the occasion. She was asked the inevitable question: "Which team [the Red Sox with Dom, or the Yanks with Joe] are you rooting for?"

Brother Tom quickly broke in with the inevitable reply: "Mother is impartial." Amen.

When they finally began to play baseball, it looked as if the Red Sox regulars might be able to spend Sunday relaxing and preparing for the Dodgers. Dominic sliced a single to right, and after Pesky forced him at second, Williams hit a rope down the right field line that Henrich managed to touch but not stop. If it had continued to the corner, it would have been a certain double,

but it plunked against the huge frame of umpire Cal Hubbard. With this generous assist from the umpire, the Yanks held Williams to a single and Pesky at second.

Reynolds wild-pitched them both up a base, and Stephens scored Pesky with a long fly to right. Allie then uncorked another wild pitch and Ted moved to third, but Reynolds struck out Doerr to end the inning. Would Ted have scored had he reached second on his hit? Twenty-five years later, Red Sox fans still speculate. At the time it didn't seem to matter for in the third the Yankees did their best to hand the game to Boston. With one out, Reynolds walked Pesky, Williams, and Stephens. Doerr punched a short single to right, scoring Pesky. Exit Reynolds; enter Joe Page.

The ace reliever must have been watching Reynolds too closely. He walked Al Zarilla and Billy Goodman, forcing in two more runs, and Boston led 4-0. On the brink of disaster, Page suddenly reversed himself and began one of his greatest clutch relief jobs. For the next 6⅔ innings (Page's longest stint of the season), Boston's total offense would be a walk, a hit batsman, and a single by Doerr.

In the meantime the Yankees touched Parnell for two runs in the fourth and two more in the fifth. The fourth run scored when Bill Johnson hit into a double play after McCarthy had replaced Parnell with Joe Dobson. Otherwise Dobson threatened to match Page's stinginess—until he faced Johnny Lindell in the eighth. Hitting .229 and without a homer since July 31, Lindell hit one into the left field stands for the game winner.

With their teams once again tied

for first, Ellis Kinder and Vic Raschi would be called upon for the most important starting assignments in their baseball careers—the last game of the 1949 season.

October 2

"Two straight seasons and one final game settles it," Birdie Tebbetts complained. "When Cronin sends my contract for next year, I'm gonna specify that I not show up until October. It's much better to play this game when you're fresh than when you're tired." Birdie would go 0 for 7 in the last two games. If they had based his next year's contract on this performance, he would have been lucky to receive a box of cigars.

The mighty mite, Phil Rizzuto, immediately brought the 70,000 fans to their feet by opening the bottom of the first with a drive down the left field line that Williams was unable to cut off. It caromed off the railing and Rizzuto had a triple. Henrich grounded out to Doerr and Rizzuto scored easily. DiMaggio then sliced a triple to right, but Kinder yielded nothing more and the Jolter died at third. For the rest of his stint, Kinder was magnificent. Only four Yankees reached first—two singles and two walks. But Raschi, too, was brilliant. Doerr and Al Zarilla reached him for Boston's first hits (singles) in the fourth, putting Red Sox on first and third with two outs, but Vic struck out Goodman, squelching the most serious Red Sox chance until the ninth.

Still trailing 1-0 in the top of the eighth, Joe McCarthy made a move that would rankle the second guessers as much as his picking of Galehouse for the playoff the previous year. With one out and the bases empty, he chose to hit for Kinder.

His candidate was rookie Tom Wright, recently brought up from Louisville, where he had hit a very respectable .307. Wright walked but Dominic could produce only a hard-hit double-play ball. Kinder was out of the game and Boston was still down a run. It is true that no matter how well Kinder would have pitched the eighth, the Red Sox *had* to get a run. But with the Boston power coming up in the ninth, McCarthy was open to criticism. Kinder would go to his grave saying, "If the old man had left me in, we would have won the pennant."

As a reliever, Mel Parnell could not make an old-timer forget "Firpo" Marberry. Henrich greeted Mel with a home run, and Berra followed with a single. Trying to cut his losses, McCarthy brought in Tex Hughson, and when Joe DiMaggio lined into a double play, it looked for a moment as if the skipper had pushed the right button this time. But Johnny Lindell singled and Hank Bauer (running for Lindell) raced to third on Bill Johnson's single to left. Cliff Mapes walked, loading the bases. Jerry Coleman then hit a slicing fly ball to right that Al Zarilla pursued as if the entire season depended on it. It did. Al dove for it, but it eluded his grasp and cleared the bases. The Red Sox came up in the ninth yearning for the one-run deficit they had the inning before. For now they trailed 5-0.

Pesky fouled out. Raschi, pitching too carefully to Williams, walked him. He advanced to second on a wild pitch and to third on Vern Stephens' single. Then Doerr reminded Joe DiMaggio that even superstars are mortal. Still recovering from a serious virus infection, Joe couldn't reach Bobby's drive over his head in center, and Doerr raced to

third with a two-run triple. Hitting triples over DiMaggio's head just wasn't done. After this one, Joe removed himself from the game.

Raschi disposed of Zarllla harmlessly, but Goodman singled, scoring Doerr. The tying run now came to the plate in the person of the admittedly weary Birdie Tebbetts. Raschi went for the outside corner, and Birdie lifted a lazy foul to Henrich. The tremendous rush the Red Sox had made the second half of the season had fallen two runs short.

In analyzing that season some 25 years later, even the most partisan Red Sox fan notices one glaring difference between the two teams. Of the 60 games in which Joe Page appeared in 1949, the Yankees won 42, lost 17, and tied 1. Boston just didn't have a stopper in the same class. Put a Dick Radatz of 1963 and 1964 on that 1949 Red Sox team, and the World Series would have been played at Fenway.

Top: fans besiege Yankee Stadium 18 hours before second game of New York-Boston season-ending series. *Above:* Casey Stengel leads the Yankees' victory chorus.

1967

There were good signs in the second half of 1966, but the Fenway faithful could be forgiven for not having noticed them. Having become accustomed, after a generation of mediocrity and worse, to reading the standings from the bottom up, they found their team after the 1966 season resting conveniently in ninth place, a scant half game from the cellar, where the once-mighty Yankees now languished. And so the fans did not notice that after August 1 the team had played its best ball in years. And when the 1967 season brought a new manager in Dick Williams, who had done well with the Boston farm team in Toronto of the International League, the fans groused, "Why doesn't Yawkey give the job to the real Williams? At least with Ted back in town we'd have some excitement."

The new manager was more hopeful. When asked in preseason to comment on his new team's chances, which the oddsmakers listed as 100-1 to win the pennant, Williams blandly predicted, "We'll win more than we'll lose." By the middle of July, after a 10-game winning streak, he had shortened and sweetened it: "We'll win." The Impossible Dream had begun to take shape.

Who were these Red Sox whom New England ignored in 1966 and adored a year later? The nucleus is easy to recall: a 22-game and Cy Young award winner, right hander Jim Lonborg; a superb hitting and fielding outfield—Triple Crown winner Carl Yastrzemski in left, explosive Reggie Smith in center, and the ill-fated Tony Conigliaro in right; a power-hitting shortstop, Rico Petrocelli; and a more likely power man

and surprisingly agile fielder, behemoth first baseman George Scott.

The supporting cast, like that of any successful production, was indispensable and forgettable: Jerry Adair and Dalton Jones, who filled in for Rico when he was injured, and for youngsters Joe Foy at third and Mike Andrews at second when they faltered; the aging Yankees star, Elston Howard, who arrived from New York in August to give the Red Sox' catchers, Mike Ryan and Russ Gibson, and the pitchers as well, a cram course in composure under pennant pressure; the mostly anonymous pitching staff that shuttled from starting to relief assignments as if there were no difference—Lee Stange, Gary ("Ding Dong") Bell, Jose Santiago, Darrell Brandon, Dave Morehead, Jerry Stephenson, and Gary Waslewski. There was a relief ace in John Wyatt, who compiled a 2.60 ERA in 60 appearances, and a budding star in rookie Sparky Lyle, but for the most part this was a pitching staff so undistinguished (for Morehead, Stephenson, and Waslewski: total starts—28, total complete games—1) that it challenged manager Williams to produce a rotation. At season's end the club's ERA was 3.35, eighth in the league. Even Lonborg, though he was superb down the stretch and in the Series, had an ERA of only 3.16. How then did the Red Sox manage to win one more and lose one less than the Tigers and Twins? On consistent and powerful hitting and that mysterious element that the truest believers call destiny and the rest of us, luck —luck that 92 wins and a .568 percentage were good enough to win this year; luck that no team caught fire in September. And now having demythicized the Impossible Dream we can relive it.

Top: Williams and Yaz exult in victory.
Bottom: Jose Santiago delivers first pitch, a strike, to Minnesota's Zoilo Versalles in first of two 1967 showdown games.

Below: reliever John Wyatt. *Opposite:* key play in September 30 game. Versalles drops throw, allowing Mike Andrews, sliding, to reach second and Jerry Adair first. Next batter, Yaz, homered.

It began at Fenway Park on opening day with a 5-4 win over Chicago. Jim Lonborg won it thanks to Rico's three-run knock into the screen. A few days later 21-year-old Billy Rohr held the Yankees hitless for 8⅔ innings at the stadium before Elston Howard singled to right center for New York's only hit in Boston's 3-0 shutout. At the beginning of the half-inning, the verdict as well as the no-hitter had seemed still in doubt. "It was [Yankees left fielder Tom] Tresh who opened the ninth with one so deep into left that I thought it was gone," recalls Yaz. "All I could think of was the kid's no-hitter. I leaped as high as I could and lost my balance coming down, but I had the ball. I may have made better catches, but I don't remember any. Rohr never did much after that, but his one game that day gave us a tremendous lift."

Yaz had become the leader the Red Sox had waited seven years for. White Sox manager Eddie Stanky (the aging "Brat") had called Yaz "a great ball player from the neck down," to which the Boston slugger responded with 6 for 9 against Chicago in a doubleheader, including a home run. As he trotted past third on the round tripper, he tipped his hat to Stanky.

Lonborg, the intellectual Stanford graduate, had changed his style. When the opposing pitcher dusted off a Red Sox batter, Jim asked Williams, "Who do you want me to get?" "No Toehold" Jim began winning impressively. In one outing he struck out 13 A's.

Not all the other players were as cooperative with the manager, but it didn't show on the field. Confirming reports that he and Williams didn't get along, Joe Foy told the press, "I'm a New York boy; maybe I should be playing down there," then hit a long grand slam at Yankee Stadium, and the Red Sox won 7-1. Tony C. had similar problems with the manager and a similar solution. Tony crashed one with two outs and one on in the bottom of the eleventh at Fenway and with the Bosox trailing 1-0. The whole team greeted him at the plate.

A writer made an amazing discovery: "Not a single member of this year's squad has ever played with a Boston team that finished over .500," he reported. To be sure, Boston was playing no better than .500 baseball at the time, but none of the other clubs was doing much better. Rico said elatedly, "This year is so different; you really look forward to coming to the ball park. It's the most exciting thing I've ever seen." In Petro's first two years, Boston had lost 190 games.

Then slump. The Sox dropped two in California and three straight at Detroit. Boston had one more with the Tigers before the All-Star break, and Williams wanted desperately to end the slide before the layoff. The

88

stretch-drive combo—Lonborg and Yaz—gave an indication of things to come. Lonborg pitched masterfully, Yaz hit a home run off Fred Gladding, and the Sox won.

After the break they rolled up a 10-game winning streak, including a doubleheader sweep of Cleveland, 8-5 and 5-1. Conigliaro hit home runs in both games, and Foy hit another grand slam. Lee ("Stringer") Stange completed five games, all victories, in July, including a month-ending whitewashing of the Twins.

In August California slumped and the field narrowed to four: Chicago, Minnesota, Detroit, and Boston. It would be six weeks before the next contender would drop out.

On August 4, Bell hit Killebrew on the arm with a pitch. Harmon had a rough week or two, and the Twins started to complain. They stopped abruptly on August 18, when the Sox lost Conigliaro for the year. "The ball seemed to follow me in," he said later of Jack Hamilton's fastball. "I didn't freeze; I jerked my head back so fast my helmet flipped off." The result was a fractured

cheekbone and a monstrous wound around the left eye. With 20 home runs already, Tony C. had seemed a sure bet for 25 or 30. Stunned and desperate at having lost the league's leading home run hitter, the Sox grabbed 11-year veteran outfielder Jim Landis, recently released by Detroit. Landis signed on August 23, hit a home run in the 7-5 win over Washington the next day, and was released on Monday, August 28.

In the meantime, A's owner Charley Finley became angry at his $22,000 first baseman-outfielder, Ken ("Hawk") Harrelson. "Charley wanted to humiliate me, so he put me on irrevocable waivers," the Hawk said. "This makes me a free agent, so I can sign wherever I want."

Ed Short, general manager of the White Sox, reported, "We offered him fifty thousand dollars and he laughed." Harrelson finally signed with Boston for between $75,000 and $150,000—accounts differed. Ken hit only .200 for the Sox in 1967, but he contributed a double, triple, and home run against the White Sox in a 10-2 Jose Santiago win on September 1. The next year he led the American League in RBIs.

A hopeful sign: In the opener of a doubleheader at Chicago on August 27, Ken Berry was on third in the last of the ninth with Boston leading 4-3. Duane Josephson was batting with one down. He lofted a fly ball to medium right, to Jose Tartabull, normally not the strongest armed of right fielders. "You've got to credit Ellie Howard," Dick Williams said. "The throw was too high and a little off line. Howard grabbed it and leaped down on Berry." Maybe the throw was off line, but pennants are not won on perfection. Rather, it seems to be disaster courted and then averted that marks the pennant winner. If so, the Sox were marked for success.

At the end of August, Yaz began his private affair with disaster. He went 0 for 18, finally forcing Williams to rest him against New York on August 30. But in the eighth inning the manager relented. Stephenson had pitched a strong seven innings, John Wyatt had replaced him in the eighth, and now Williams needed a man who could hit the game breaker. Three innings later, Carl delivered it, and Boston had a crucial 2-1 win over Al Downing.

Three straight losses at the beginning of September suppressed New England's pennant fever temporarily. Then Carl hit two against Washington on the fifth and the Dream seemed attainable again.

With one week to go, the same four teams that had battled each other since August were still vying for the crown: Boston and Minnesota, tied for first at 90-68; Chicago, a game behind at 89-69; and Detroit, a game and a half behind at 88-69. Dick Williams recounted the prelude to the frantic ending: "Joe Adcock brings Cleveland into Fenway on Tuesday and Wednesday, and they beat us two straight. We have two days off and are due to play Minnesota on Saturday and Sunday in Boston. It looks like we're out of it. [Minnesota has split two with California; Detroit has taken one from New York.] In the meantime the White Sox have gone into Kansas City for a Wednesday doubleheader. They go against [Pat] Dobson and [Jim] Hunter and lose them both. This really shakes them up, and they drop the next three games to Washington and are the first ones to fold.

"So, [at 90-70] we're one game away from Minnesota [91-69] and even with Detroit [89-69], but the Tigers have played two games less and are one game ahead of us in the loss column. If they win all their [four] games, they'll beat us no matter what we do. And we still have to beat Minnesota both games. Then we get a break. It rains both Thursday and Friday in Detroit, and the Tigers have to play a doubleheader against California Saturday and Sunday."

Thus began the two most important days for the Red Sox since 1949—Saturday, September 30, and Sunday, October 1. "Of course we were nervous, particularly Thursday and Friday when we were waiting," says Yaz, "but it had been like this for three months. Naturally the same holds true for both Minnesota and Detroit."

Both Minnesota and Boston had had two days of rest, so the managers could use the pitchers they wanted—Jim Kaat for Minnesota, Jose Santiago for Boston. "Why Santiago and not Lonborg?" the fans asked.

"What difference does it make?" Williams retorted. "We have to win them both."

Jim Lonborg hurls pennant clincher. He allowed three runs, but Sox prevailed 5-3.

Minnesota was on the board almost at the start. Zoilo Versalles led off with a single, Cesar Tovar flied out, Killebrew walked, and Tony Oliva singled home Versalles. But Santiago was pitching well and retired both Rod Carew and Ted Uhlaender on grounders. In the third the game changed radically but for the moment imperceptibly. In pitching to Santiago, Kaat heard something pop in his elbow. "The whole arm felt weak as I tried to pitch to Andrews [the next batter]," explained Kaat. Minnesota's best pitcher in the stretch was through for the day.

In came Jim Perry, long-time Red Sox nemesis. ("Our players change, but Jim Perry can still beat us."— Tom Yawkey.) Perry walked Mike Andrews. Adair grounded out, moving Andrews to second. As Yaz strode to the plate, the full house came to life, only to sulk as Yaz fanned, but once again the significance of the play on the field had escaped them. "He threw me a slider that really didn't break," Yaz recalls. "He struck me out, but I knew he didn't have it."

Two innings later it became clear. Reggie Smith opened the fifth with a double, and Williams sent up Dalton Jones to hit for Russ Gibson. Jones scratched an infield single, moving Smith to third. Perry struck out Santiago and Andrews, but Jerry Adair nullified all Perry's work by singling to right, scoring Smith, tying the game 1-1, and moving Jones to third. Yaz broke the tie with a bullet between first and second. Second baseman Rod Carew made a marvelous stop in short right field, only to find that no one had covered first. Yaz had a single, and the Sox led 2-1.

The Twins tied it again in the top of the sixth, but George Scott greeted reliever Ron Kline with a long home run into the center field bleachers in the bottom of the frame. Jose put the Twins down in order in the top of the seventh, and good things happened to Boston in the bottom half. Mike Andrews managed a check-swing infield hit. Adair followed with a come-backer to Kline, who threw to Versalles hoping to start a twin killing, but the shortstop dropped the ball and instead of nobody on and two down, Boston had runners on first and second with no outs. Twins manager Cal Ermer rushed in left hander Jim Merritt to face Yaz, but this superstar had no patience for lefty-right games. Yaz put one of Merritt's pitches in the bullpen, and it was 6-2, Boston. It was Carl's forty-fourth home run of the year, putting him first in the league and second only to Foxx for home runs by a Boston player in a season. More importantly, it pulled Boston into a first-place tie with the Twins.

Minnesota scared the Red Sox in the ninth when Killebrew hit a two-

91

out, two-run homer off reliever Gary Bell. Fortunately, Adair grabbed Tony Oliva's line drive, and Boston had the final out. Killebrew's homer had tied the Minnesota strong man with Yaz for the league lead, jeopardizing Carl's run for the Triple Crown. After the game Williams admitted to Yaz, "I called the fastball for Harmon, Carl; we just couldn't walk him."

Carl desperately wanted the Triple Crown, but he replied, "It was the right move; you certainly didn't want to walk him with a four-run lead." The pennant came first.

Detroit had won its first game but had lost the second. At the close of play, Boston and Minnesota were tied for first at 91-70, Detroit was a half-game behind at 90-70.

After the first 161 games of 1967 had eliminated only seven of ten teams it was incomprehensible that the last game would be a dud, no matter who won it. And it surely wasn't. The two best pitchers in the league—Jim Lonborg and Dean Chance—faced each other for the pennant or, at worst, the right to meet Detroit in a playoff.

As in the first game, the Twins broke first. They scored on Oliva's double in the first and a costly error by Yaz in the third.

Then came the Boston sixth, probably the most illustrious Red Sox frame since the inning 55 years earlier in which Snodgrass dropped the fly ball. Lonborg opened it by startling the Twins, the Red Sox, the 35,770 fans at the park, and the millions watching on TV. He bunted. He later explained, "Chance falls off the mound when he pitches, and Tovar was playing deep. Besides, the last thing they expected was a bunt." It worked. Adair and Jones then singled, and the bases were loaded for Frank Merriwell. Yaz

came through handsomely if not spectacularly with a single up the middle, scoring Lonnie and Adair, sending Jones to third, and tying the score. Hawk Harrelson then banged one at Zoilo, who made the mistake of his life—he threw home. Jones was safe, Yaz was on second, Harrelson was on first, and Al Worthington was on the mound. "Chance not only left the game, but he left the ball park and headed for Ohio," Dick Williams remembers with perhaps more than a trace of wishful thinking.

Worthington struck out George Scott, but he also threw two wild pitches, on one of which Yaz scored what later proved to be the winning run. Harrelson tallied the fifth run of the inning on Killebrew's error, and Boston led 5-2.

The Red Sox' superman in left field worked his magic with two outs, Oliva on first, and Killebrew on second in the eighth. Bob Allison hit a screamer into the left field corner. Killebrew scored and Oliva rounded third. "I could see what was going on, but I couldn't stop to think much," recalls Yaz. "I knew Allison was not fast, and he probably figured I'd go home to try and stop Oliva; I stuck my foot against the wall and threw to second." A run scored, narrowing the lead to 5-3, but Allison was nailed at second and the inning was over. The Sox needed only three more outs.

Ted Uhlaender opened the Twins' ninth with a single, but Rod Carew hit into a double play. Rich Rollins hit for former Boston catcher Russ Nixon and popped high to Petrocelli. The Red Sox were alone in first place.

"If they [the Tigers] win, we have to go to Detroit," explained Dick Williams in the mad clubhouse after-

After 21 years, New England has a pennant winner. Fans, most of them too young to remember the last one, mob hero Lonborg. At lower right, Ellie Howard, no stranger to pennant winning, departs quietly.

ward. "I'm going to go with Lee Stange for the playoff."

At first it seemed as if there would be one. "I wish that goddamned [Ernie] Harwell [Detroit's announcer] didn't sound so happy," yelled one player as the play-by-play broadcast reported the Tigers ahead.

Then California tied it and jumped ahead. Three hours after the Red Sox had beaten Minnesota, Dick McAuliffe hit into a double play at Detroit, and the Impossible Dream was no longer fantasy. "I haven't had a drink in four years, but I'll have one now," gushed Tom Yawkey. For the first time in 21 years, the Red Sox had won a pennant.

The World Series

It must be said at the outset that the St. Louis Cardinals were the better team in the 1967 World Series. The Cards had coasted home by 10½ games, winning 101 in all, while the Bosox, with 92 wins, had barely clawed their way to a 1-game edge

over the American League field. But Boston brought adrenalin as well as near exhaustion from the grueling pennant fight into the World Series, and after 7 games little separated the clubs but their star pitchers— well-rested, fireballing Bob Gibson of the Redbirds and bedraggled, game but plainly faltering Jim Lonborg of the Red Sox. In the seventh game Gibson bested Lonborg and left the Red Sox with only their Impossible Dream, not a postseason miracle, to savor. "It was really anticlimactic," said Yaz, who with 10 for 25 did his best to make it otherwise.

Two days after the pennant clincher, the Series began in Boston with Gibson throttling the Sox 2-1 on 6 hits. The score was closer than it should have been. St. Louis touched Boston pitching for 10 hits and numerous scoring opportunities, most of which were squandered. Meanwhile, Boston for the most part went down docilely before Gibson's fastball. Pitcher Jose Santiago lifted one into the screen in the third, tying the score at 1-1 before the Cards

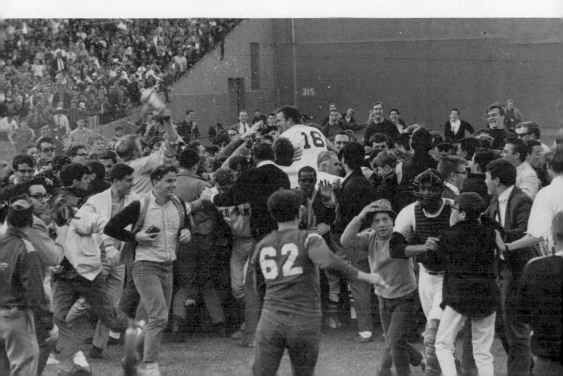

won it in the seventh. Lou Brock singled, stole second (one of his seven stolen bases in the Series), moved to third on Curt Flood's grounder, and scored as Roger Maris bounced out to second.

The next day the Bosox showed St. Louis how they had gotten this far. For 6⅔ innings Lonborg allowed not one Redbird to perch on base. Flood broke the spell with a walk, and an inning later Julian Javier ruined the no-hitter with a double, but by then Yaz had made his mark at the plate (with two solo homers), and Boston breezed 5-0.

In St. Louis for games three and four, the Red Sox were beaten at the outset of both. In game three starter Gary Bell survived only two innings, in game four Jose Santiago not even one. The Cardinals took Boston 5-2 and 6-0 (the latter triumph á five-hit Bob Gibson shutout). Down 3-1 in games, the Red Sox seemed as if they would surrender the Series with hardly a struggle.

They might have had it not been for their year-long stopper, Lonborg. The big right hander allowed only three hits (for a grand total of four in 18 Series innings) and won 3-1. Only Roger Maris' homer in the ninth marred the shutout.

Another full house greeted the Red Sox as they returned to Fenway for game six. Dick Williams got six good innings from surprise starter Gary Waslewski, and the Red Sox' bats, dormant since game two, were suddenly revitalized. In the second Rico sent one into the screen, and in the fourth the heart of the order—Yaz, Reggie, and Rico—pumped three more balls to the outer reaches of a by now pulsating Fenway. A Cardinals rally in the seventh tied the game at 4-4, but the Sox erupted for four in the bottom of the frame and

In the Series the Sox encountered hot
Lou Brock—batting against Lonborg *(left)*,
stealing second while Petrocelli awaits
throw *(below)*. As always, Yaz powered Red
Sox. *Opposite:* he connects off Dick Hughes.

the Series was tied. Now if only they could beat Gibson.

A year later, in a nearly identical situation, Curt Flood would fall down, misplaying a fly ball into a run-scoring triple that doomed the man who until that moment had seemed nearly invincible in Series competition. But this was a year earlier and instead of a strong Mickey Lolich, the Red Sox had only a battered Jim Lonborg to send against the towering Gibson. It was Jim's second start in three days, his fourth critical one in eleven, and this time it wasn't close. The Cards bombed Jim for 10 hits in six innings and a 7-1 lead by the time he departed. Boston managed a run in the eighth, but the end was clearly at hand.

Never has there been such a rousing funeral. As their heroes came to bat in the ninth, the patrons were on their feet in salute. Years later, Tom Yawkey recaptured those feelings of supercharged loyalty to the Red Sox. "No, I can't say the World Series of sixty-seven was a great disappointment," he mused, "not after the great year they gave us."

MOMENTS
TO REMEMBER

The Pennant on a Wild Pitch

Young John Taylor was a habitué of the fleshpots of Boston, and his father, General Charles Taylor, a proper Bostonian, worried about it. He felt that his son needed a more respectable diversion, and so after the 1903 season, the old soldier bought the world champion Boston Pilgrims for him. Young John took his new responsibility very seriously, even to the point of ensuring that the newspaper Dad owned, the Boston *Globe* received no special favors in covering the team.

With the support of his father, the younger Taylor was in a good position to be scrupulous. When the General acquired the club, the *Globe*'s renowned sportswriter, Tim Murnane, who had initially reacted coolly to Boston's American League entry, suddenly became an enthusiastic Pilgrims partisan. And it was a club worthy of enthusiasm—the same club basically in 1904 as the one that had beaten Pittsburgh in the World Series the year before. One 20-game winner, Long Tom Hughes, had gone to Washington, but another, Jesse Tannehill, had come from the New York Highlanders.

Unlike 1903, when the Pilgrims swept to the American League pennant, the 1904 race was hotly contested from the start. The early challengers included the White Sox, Indians (paced by Woonsocket, Rhode Island's hero, Nap LaJoie), and Athletics, with their immodest pitching great, Rube Waddell.

On May 1, Waddell opened a five-game series at Boston by holding the Pilgrims to one hit in besting Tannehill 3-0. When Rube's turn to pitch came around again in the last

game of the series, on May 5, he faced his rival, Cy Young, and boasted, "I'll give you the same what I give Tannehill!" The Farmer replied to the challenge with the first perfect game in American League history. "I don't think I ever had more stuff than that day," he said with a glow after his 3-0 triumph. "And my speed was as fast as ever."

By September, the race had narrowed to Boston and New York. The Pilgrims had helped the Highlanders when on June 19 they traded outfielder Patsy Dougherty to New York for utility infielder Bob Unglaub— the first of many disastrous Boston trades through the years. While Patsy led the league in runs in 1904, Unglaub played in all of seven games for Boston.

The leader of the Highlanders was a grouchy spitballer from western Massachusetts, "Happy Jack" Chesbro. In 1904, he would win 41 games, still the all-time modern single-season record, and come as close as anyone can to pitching a team to the pennant. On October 7, in the opening game of the final series of the season, Chesbro beat Boston in New York 3-2, giving the Highlanders a half-game lead, but the next day the Pilgrims swept a doubleheader from the Highlanders in Boston, 13-2 and 1-0. Thus, with only a final doubleheader left, to be played in New York on Monday, October 10, the Pilgrims had to win only one to clinch the pennant.

To the Highlanders, winning the pennant was crucial. Only two years before they had moved north from Baltimore in an attempt to shed their image as the last-place Orioles. Now they had, and they boasted some fine players—in addition to Chesbro and Dougherty, Wee Willie Keeler, perhaps the finest place hitter of all time; 23-game winner Jake Powell; and the intemperate but accomplished shortstop, "the Tabasco Kid," Kid Elberfeld. But in contrast to the Pilgrims, who now dominated baseball in Boston, the Highlanders were still outdrawn and, many said, outclassed in New York by John McGraw's Giants of the National League. Now the newcomers had a chance to win a pennant over the team that had the year before beaten the best in the National League. If they could, their gain—in respectability and thus at the gate—would be substantial.

The Highlanders' little park could seat only 12,000, but the New York papers reported that 28,540 spectators attended the season's finale. The papers generously overestimated the crowd, though it stood 15 deep along the fringes of the large outfield, which had to be roped off. Among the standees was the ever-present Nuff Ced McGreevey and several other Royal Rooters.

New York struck first, picking up two runs in the fifth. Catcher Red Kleinow singled to left, and Chesbro mashed a base hit off pitcher Bill Dineen's chest. When Patsy Dougherty singled up the middle, scoring Kleinow and sending Chesbro to third, Nuff Ced turned to the Rooters and exclaimed, "Let's pass the hat. Maybe we can get Taylor to buy back Patsy." Before Dineen retired the side, he had walked Keeler and Elberfeld, forcing in another run.

Boston tied it in the seventh with two cheapies. Candy LaChance beat out an infield grounder, and Hobe Ferris bounced an elusive ground ball just out of the reach of second baseman Jim Williams. Lou Criger sacrificed, putting both runners in scoring position. Dineen then grounded to Williams, but in his haste to nail LaChance at the plate, the second baseman threw wildly, and both Candy and Ferris scored. It stayed tied until the ninth.

The famous (or, if you are a Chesbro fan, infamous) final inning opened with an infield bleeder that Lou Criger beat out for a single. Dineen bunted him to second, and outfielder Kip Selbach moved him to third by grounding out behind the runner. Then with two outs and Freddy Parent at the plate, Jack must have really moistened one. The pitch soared past catcher Kleinow and Criger scored easily. Dineen handled New York effortlessly in the ninth, and Boston had won its second flag in a row.

Unfortunately, there would be no World Series this year. After the veteran carouser, John Taylor, threw a wild party for the players and Rooters at the Hotel Putnam in Boston, the Pilgrims challenged the National League champion Giants only to receive this terse insult in reply: "We don't play minor leaguers." So the Pilgrims would have to wait eight years (by which time they had changed their name to the Red Sox) before purging the Giants of their arrogance.

With no World Series to remember for that year, baseball historians have focused on the pitch that gave the Pilgrims the pennant. Was it a wild pitch, as the official scorer ruled, or a passed ball? Chesbro claimed long afterward that "Kleinow should have caught it," and after Chesbro died, his widow spent almost the rest of her life trying to have the official scoring changed. But more objective observers upheld the ruling. When baseball writer Fred Lieb asked Kid Elberfeld in 1942 whether the scoring should be reversed, the old Highlander replied, "Hell no, Fred, that ball rode so far over Kleinow's head he couldn't have caught it standing on a stepladder."

"It Could Have Been Called Either Way"

Usually, the decisions of the official scorer are of interest to few besides the players involved. What does it matter, for example, if Boston won in 1904 on a wild pitch or a passed ball? But when there is a record at stake, particularly one so important that baseball fans and officials alike could not suffer for it to be tarnished by inaccuracy, then the official scorer becomes more than the petty bookkeeper whose ledger-keeping may annoy the employees or even the boss, but rarely

the customers. He becomes a tyrant-accountant, whose crediting of one man's account and debiting of another's becomes a matter of justice. And if he is wrong?

On September 11, 1923, justice was in the hands of Fred Lieb, and he ruled "hit" where he might have ruled "error." A storm of protest raged briefly over his decision, but it was soon accepted, and thus the truth was buried in a ledger that now no one reopens but the most dedicated baseball historians and the most diehard Red Sox fans. And so it continues to be commonly accepted that the only man to pitch two consecutive no-hitters was Johnny Vander Meer of Cincinnati, on June 11 and 15, 1938, and it is all but forgotten that the Red Sox' Howard Ehmke did it too—15 years earlier—only the official scorer didn't agree.

On September 7, 1923, Ehmke had pitched a no-hitter against the Philadelphia Athletics. It was a fine

Howard Ehmke as a member of the Red
Sox, *top;* as a Detroit Tiger, *above.*

performance but something less than an immortal feat inasmuch as "Sad Sam" Jones of the Yankees had done the exact same thing three days before. The Athletics at the beginning of the twenties were light-years away from the powerful Athletics of the end of the decade.

In his next start Ehmke faced considerably stronger opposition—the New York Yankees and the beginning of Murderers' Row. The Yanks boasted an outfield of .300 hitters (Babe Ruth, .393; Bob Meusel, .313; and Whitey Witt, .314) and an infield only slightly less menacing: Wally Pipp, .304; Joe Dugan, .283; Aaron Ward, .284; and Wally Schang, .276. Only Everett Scott at .246 was a relatively easy out, at least by 1923 standards. On September 11, 1923, pitching against young George Pipgras, Ehmke faced that awesome lineup in Yankee Stadium, and stunned the 15,000 fans who, bored with a pennant race the Yanks had all but clinched, had probably come to see the Big Guy bring no-hit Ehmke back down to earth.

To open the game, Whitey Witt bounced a sharp grounder at Howard Shanks, the Boston third baseman. The ball bounced perfectly at Shanks, but hit him in the chest and rolled toward second base. Before Shanks could retrieve the ball, Witt, a fast man, had beaten the throw to first base.

—New York *Times* 9/12/23

It was the writers' consensus of opinion that if the play had occurred after the fifth inning, Shanks would have been given an error. But in view of Ehmke's previous nine innings, why didn't the scorer give him the benefit of a doubt at the beginning? Fred Lieb was no neophyte. He was 'one of the great baseball writers of all time, and surely he knew that no-hitters, much less double no-hitters, oughtn't be kicked away like ground balls.

Lieb offered the following defense: "I took into consideration that Shanks, an outfielder by trade, had played the ball clumsily, but also that Witt, a left-handed batsman, was a streak of lightning going down to first."

As the game progressed, the fans didn't realize that Lieb had scored Witt's ground ball a hit, so they became increasingly excited as each batter went down. Only two days before, on his first start since his no-hitter, Sam Jones had gone until the seventh inning before allowing a hit. The stadium customers were now witnessing a second attempt at baseball's first double no-hitter, and they responded enthusiastically when two outstanding fielding plays saved Ehmke. In the sixth, George Pipgras, pitching a great game at this point himself, shot a ground ball up the middle, but second baseman Norm McMillan grabbed it with his bare hand and threw out George by a step. Earlier in the game, Ira Flagstead (there's a name for old Red Sox fans) had robbed Joe Dugan with a splendid running catch.

In the eighth Ehmke saved himself. After Aaron Ward had been hit by a pitch, Deacon Scott slammed one back at Ehmke. Howard knocked it down in self-defense, then whipped it to second, starting a double play. In the ninth, each out was greatly applauded, and when the game ended the fans rushed out on the field to mob Ehmke. They were convinced that they had seen Howard's second no-hitter in a row. Only later did Lieb's ruling become widely known, and by then it was too late for the vehement outcry to do any good.

Joe Tinker, who had been at the game visiting with Frank Chance, Boston's manager and Tinker's own former mentor, commented bluntly when asked about the play. "No question, it was an error all the way. Ehmke was robbed," he said. Chance, on the other hand, was tactful to the point of evasiveness. "It was a close one—you could have called it either way—but I sure feel sorry for Howard," he mused. Umpire Tommy Connally candidly agreed with Tinker. "I saw it perfectly and it was unquestionably an error."

A group of Ehmke's baseball friends circulated a petition and presented it to Ban Johnson with a request that he reverse Lieb's decision, but Ban turned them down.

Without doubt Lieb called it the way he saw it, but he was far too conscientious to ignore the criticisms. Several years later, when Shanks was traded to the Yankees, he told Lieb, "Fred, I think it should have been scored an error." Lieb has written: "Ever since Shanks told me that, I've had the play on my conscience."

Who knows what weighs a scorer's decision? Perhaps the next inning he would have called it an error. If he had, Howard Ehmke would be in the record book and Johnny Vander Meer would be an also-ran. But then baseball would have lost a fascinating dramatization of its clumsy system of justice. Perhaps Fred Lieb's decision was a healthy one after all.

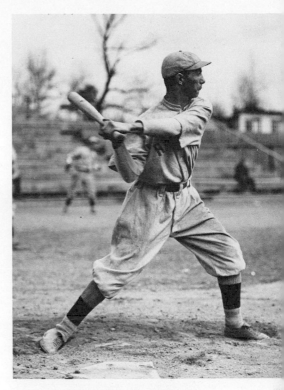

The weakest hitter in the Yankees' lineup that Ehmke faced was Deacon Scott, but in the eighth inning of the near second no-hitter, he hit a hard shot—a comebacker that Ehmke turned into a double play.

The Big Sweep

All middle-aged Red Sox fans remember the 5-game sweep of the Yankees in the torrid New York of July 1939. How can one forget winning 5 in a row from a team that would itself win 106 games and take the pennant by 17? And yet the faithful have tampered with the legend. There are ardent Red Sox fans who swear that the sweep began on the Fourth of July, when actually it started three days later; the 12-game winning streak, of which these 5 were the heart, began on the Fourth. Others claim to remember that Jim Tabor of the Red Sox hit "all those home runs" off the Yankees, when actually he did it earlier in the year off the Athletics. Still others say they recall that Tex Hughson won one of the games (though he didn't join the team until 1941) or that Ben Chapman hit a home run (though he was playing for Cleveland at the time).

Apparently not even a fantasy-come-true can escape the distortions of oral history. So here is what happened, recorded in the belief that this is one legend that needs no embellishment.

July 7

Brutally hot weather and an 11½-game New York lead over the second-place Red Sox persuaded Yankees manager Joe McCarthy to keep to his hotel room that afternoon. After all, the pennant was all but decided, and Joe had more important things on his mind than the Red Sox. The All-Star Game was to be played at Yankee Stadium on the eleventh, and he would be managing the American League squad, for which nine of his Yankees had been selected. Naturally he wanted to look good. So today he left the Yankees on their own, no doubt confident that his pitching choice, Red Ruffing, would stifle the Sox' bats and that the Yankees' hitters would pummel Boston's Jake Wade as Max Baer had Primo Carnera. However, the Yankees' ace would prove to be mortal and "Whistlin' Jake" not quite the lantern jaw.

The start of the game was delayed when a group of well-wishers from Hoboken, New Jersey, presented Boston utility infielder Tom Carey with a suitcase. Receiving the gift would be Carey's sole distinguishing mark in the series until the fifth game, when he too strenuously protested a call and was thrown out of a game he had never entered.

The Red Sox reached Ruffing for a run in the first when Doc Cramer singled, went to second on a walk to Jimmie Foxx, and scored on manager Joe Cronin's base hit. But the Yankees tied it in the second. In the third, the hot weather seemed to lower the boiling points of the Sox and, according to them, impair the judgment of the sweltering gentlemen in blue. Umpires Kollis and Summers changed their call from safe to out on a line drive Cramer hit to Yankees second baseman Joe Gordon. Cronin charged out of the dugout and bounced from one umpire to another in a furious but vain attempt to overturn the reversal. He was still fuming when he came to bat in the fourth, but this time he found a more accommodating object for his wrath—the ball. He pasted one of Ruffing's pitches into the right field stands, and the Red Sox led 2-1. Once again New York tied it, Joe DiMaggio singling home Red Rolfe in the bottom of the fourth.

Heroes of the Big Sweep: *left*, Roger ("Doc")
Cramer; *center*, Fritz Ostermueller; *right*,
Jimmie Foxx, posed here with Hal Trosky.

105

Foxx's double and Williams' single in the fifth gave the Red Sox the lead for the third time, but in the sixth the Yankees came back for the third time, evening the score on Gordon's double. Had Emerson Dickman, who replaced Wade, not struck out Babe Dahlgren and Ruffing at this point, the Yankees might have broken open the game and aborted the winning streak.

In the eighth the Red Sox finally scored an unanswered run. Williams singled, Cronin walked, and Ruffing hit Joe Vosmik. Then Jim Tabor barely beat the relay on a near double-play grounder, and Williams scored the winning run in a 4-3 victory. Joe McCarthy considered his 10½-game lead and joked, "This is too close for comfort." But he was at the park for the doubleheader the next day.

July 8

The city was still sweltering as the two teams squared off for a Saturday twin bill. Once again the start was slightly delayed, this time by a mass invasion of Japanese beetles.

In the first game Boston's Fritz Ostermueller worked against Oral Hildebrand. Fritz was one of a seemingly limitless number of Red Sox pitchers who seemed uncommonly talented in intermittent streaks but failed to fulfill their promise over an extended period. This was one of his good days. He limited the power-laden "Bronx Bombers" to four hits, and Boston blasted Hildebrand for eight in the first four innings, including doubles by Cramer, Foxx, and Williams. Only a tremendous throw by Joe DiMaggio that nailed Tabor at third in the second and Joe's outstanding catch on Tabor in the third kept the game close. At

106

Clockwise from left: Joe Vosmik; Boston's three catchers: Johnny Peacock, left, Moe Berg, and Gene Desautels; and aging Lefty Grove. Of Berg, a linguist and intellectual but no star, it was said, "He can speak nine languages and can't hit in any of them."

the finish it was 3-1, Boston, the Sox' second straight over New York at the stadium. There have been Boston teams that would have considered that accomplishment a miracle in itself.

In the nightcap, Cronin opened with Denny Galehouse against Yankees rookie Marius Russo. For the first six innings it was a pitcher's duel. Russo did not even allow a hit, allowing the Sox only a walk to Cronin.

In the seventh, Foxx, who had twice been called out on strikes, rammed a one-out single. Ted Williams grounded out, moving "Double X" to second. Cronin then drilled a single to left, scoring Foxx.

Two singles and a sacrifice fly produced a run in the Yankees' half. Then Joe Gordon attempted to steal second but the throw from catcher Gene Desautels cut him down. "Flash" raged at the call, but umpire Bill Summers took the weather into account, at least for the moment, and walked away. Unfortunately, after Tabor opened the Boston eighth with a walk, Gordon decided to continue to berate Summers and finally provoked the ump into throwing him out. Tabor then added injury to insult by stealing second, and the Yankees' dugout erupted in frustration. Both Lefty Gomez and Jake Powell (neither in the game) were canned. Even the fast-failing captain, Lou Gehrig, was seen to rattle a bat in the dugout, but as a venerated elder statesman, he enjoyed a certain immunity from umpires' reprisals. The game resumed. Russo retired Desautels and Galehouse, but the ever-dependable Doerr doubled home Tabor, putting Boston in front 2-1.

After an unproductive pinch hitter replaced Marius at the plate in the eighth, "Grandma" Johnny Murphy relieved for New York for the second time that day. Foxx greeted him with a blast into the lower right field stands, a homer that proved to be a vital insurance run when the Yankees scored in the ninth. That rally fell one run short, mainly because Bobby Doerr made a great stop on Charlie Keller, and Boston triumphed 3-2.

The word went out from Connecticut to Maine: the Red Sox had knocked off the hated Yankees three straight at the stadium, and there would be another doubleheader the next day. "Just who the hell are supposed to be the world champions, us or the Red Sox?" growled McCarthy.

July 9

For Saturday's doubleheader 27,000 people had come to the stadium; Sunday's drew close to 50,000. The New York *Times* reported: "The crowd cheered mainly for the Red Sox at every turn." No doubt many New Englanders changed their Sunday plans on Saturday night and headed for New York. Under ordinary circumstances a Red Sox fan can find better things to do on the weekend than subject himself to the inferno of Yankee Stadium in the middle of a heat wave. But to the truly committed, beating the Yankees makes a heat wave incidental.

Two of the greatest left handers in the American League, Lefty Gomez and Lefty Grove, started the first game. Such a pairing seven or eight years before may have produced a pitching masterpiece, but by July 1939, both pitchers were in decline and this day neither could last past the sixth.

The Yankees scored a run in the second inning and two in the fourth.

Singles by Cronin, Vosmik, and Tabor produced a run for Boston in the fourth. In the fifth Jimmie Foxx hit a mammoth triple past the center field flagpole and scored, narrowing the New York margin to 3-2, as Rolfe threw out Williams.

By the seventh Emerson Dickman had replaced Grove, and Monte Pearson had relieved Gomez. In the eighth Foxx hit into a double play, erasing Doc Cramer, who had led off the inning by beating out an infield hit. (He was always doing that.) Ted Williams drew a walk (did "Colonel" Egan damn him for that?), and Cronin banged one into the left field seats for a 4-3 lead. Dickman mopped up as effectively as he had on Friday, and suddenly people began groping for record books. When was the last time Boston had won four straight at Yankee Stadium? "Didn't they do it back when Frank Chance was manager [1923]?" an announcer ventured. No one truly knew or cared; in the headiness of the moment, Red Sox fans could think of nothing but the giant-killing ahead for their heroes in game two.

For New York it was Bump Hadley (a Lynn, Massachusetts, boy gone astray) and for Boston, Eldon Auker. The submarining Auker was one of many pitchers who pitched far better against the Red Sox than for them. Today the Yankees kayoed him in the second inning, at which point "Black Jack" Wilson relieved and, it turned out, rescued him, keeping the score at 1-0 by pitching five very strong innings.

Boston tied the score with a cheapie in the fifth. Johnny Peacock (a better catcher than he ever got credit for) singled with one out. When Wilson bunted, Hadley wheeled and threw to second, hoping to nip Peacock, but Johnny beat the throw.

Doerr then rapped to the box, and this time Bump's throw to second flew into center field and Peacock scored.

Hadley's miseries continued into the sixth. Ted Williams followed a lead-off walk to Foxx with a single. Cronin bunted them along. McCarthy played the book, ordering Hadley to walk Vosmik to load the bases. Peacock hit a dribbler to Hadley, but hurrying his throw to first baseman Dahlgren, Bump heaved it into right field, and both Foxx and Williams scored. It was now 3-1, Boston.

New York brought in the sensational young Atley Donald (who would win 12 straight in 1939), and he put the fire out, striking out Vosmik on three pitches with the bases loaded. But in the eighth the Red Sox were at it again. Cramer beat out a roller and Foxx poled one into the left field stands for a 5-1 lead.

When Wilson weakened in the bottom of the inning, allowing two runs, Joe Heving replaced him. Boston fans who used to celebrate his particularly inspiring victories with the cry, "All this and Heving, too!" had the perfect occasion to use the slogan. The Yankees had thrown all they had at Boston to no avail.

Of course in the end the Boston upsets all went for naught. New York would win 106 and lose only 45, easily winning the pennant. Nonetheless, middle-aged Red Sox fans of today fervently (if not always accurately) recall those three days of glory with a nostalgia barely lessened by Boston's distant second-place finish. For fans who have long since become accustomed to their heroes losing pennant races, the memory of the Sox beating the perennial pennant winners 5 straight is enough to make those not-so-good old days seem golden.

"The Kid" Refuses to Back into .400

A .3995 batting average will always round out to .400, except for Theodore Samuel Williams.

Time has mellowed many bitter feelings and dulled certain feuds in the decade and a half since Ted Williams last stepped into the batter's box at Fenway. Some of the Boston papers and many of the writers who blasted Ted are gone. In place of the controversy, there remains the memory of a man with uncommon fortitude, particularly on a day in Philadelphia when he refused to miss what could have been a meaningless doubleheader.

The struggle had lasted all year, as it does for any player who strives to reach .400. The man who aims for .300 or even .350 can probably survive a prolonged slump during the season. A long dry spell is almost always fatal if one wants to enter the charmed circle of .400. As the season progresses, the chase intensifies. On the first of May it often happens that someone (Rod Carew in 1974, for example) is above the magic figure. If he is there in the middle of June, serious fans take special notice, and if he is still there on the Fourth of July, he becomes a bona fide contender. A three-day slump after the All-Star break and he's counted out. A quick spree and the pressure returns.

It's simple arithmetic. To bat .400, you must hit safely four of every ten at-bats. To reach .300 you need one hit in ten less. But bare statistics don't adequately measure the biggest requirement: utter, demanding

consistency through the devastating grind of a major league season. In New England it means being ready every day from the days when the snow (most of it, anyway) has just melted to the day when it's almost ready to return. This was the struggle of 23-year-old Ted Williams in 1941.

The year would not be a bad one for the Red Sox, but as usual the Yankees were better. The Sox would end up in second place, some 17 games behind the Yankees. Before the end of July, New York had a 7-game lead. They clinched the pennant on September 4.

The runaway race gave Ted the important advantage, particularly toward the end of the season, of not having the added pressure of a pennant race. It is interesting to note that no player in this century has batted .400 on a pennant-winning club. The double-edged pressure of both reaching .400 and contributing to a pennant quest evidently becomes an unbearable load.

Another advantage for Ted was playing in Fenway Park, not, as many believe, because of its short left

field wall—the long right field compensates for it, especially for a left-handed batter like Williams—but for owner Tom Yawkey's decision to keep advertisements off the outfield wall, thereby maintaining a solid green background for a hitter as he followed the pitch. In addition Fenway Park favors a hitter with stands that hug the foul lines and swallow up many foul balls that would be caught in other parks. It has been said that there are more new lives in Fenway than at a revival meeting.

Did Williams have another advantage—was it a hitter's year? Yes and no. In 1941, four of the teams had higher batting averages than the pre-vious year and four had lower ones. It was certainly a hitter's year compared to 1967, when Carl Yastrzemski led the American League with a .301 average, but certainly not a hitter's year compared to the National League's 1931 season, when Bill Terry hit .401 and Fred Lindstrom finished fifth in the batting race with .379.

Ted himself has acknowledged that he got a lucky break in the first part of the year. Sliding into second base during spring training, he chipped a bone in his ankle, so for the first two weeks of the regular season he did nothing but pinch hit. It almost certainly worked to the ad-

111

vantage of a man who claimed he "never hit as well in cold weather as in the dead of summer—never."

Joe Dobson had recently been obtained from Cleveland. He would eventually win more than 100 games for the Sox (and thereby join a very select list), but at this point he was not pitching regularly. So every morning he would pitch to Ted. Williams would later say, "I got the most batting practice of my life, and the best, because Dobson had a hell of a curve and a good overhand fastball, and he always bore down."

Another's extraordinary feat during that season may also have helped Williams by diverting some public attention. On May 15, 1941, Joe DiMaggio began one of the most amazing hitting streaks in baseball history. He would not go hitless in a game until July 17—56 games later. In the middle of his skein, Lou Gehrig died, and the baseball writers had yet another big story to cover. Ted had grabbed the headlines on July 8 when he belted one out of Briggs Stadium in Detroit to win the All-Star Game, but it wasn't until the last part of July that the focus shifted to his batting average.

Williams had reached the high water mark of .436 in June. By late August he was at .402 and flirting with disaster. Now the whole baseball world was watching, most of it sympathetically. He had never been as big a hero in New York as he was elsewhere (New York was DiMaggio country), but they booed Lefty Gomez at Yankee Stadium for walking Ted after he got three straight hits.

When the Red Sox visited Detroit (and Ted's favorite park), the late Harry Heilmann, then broadcasting Tigers games, advised, "Now forget about that short fence. Just hit the ball where you want it; hit your pitch;

get those base hits. You can hit .400. You can do it." Harry had been the last American Leaguer to hit .400, 18 years before.

A man who had barely missed the .400 mark four times (.384, .392, .381, and .390), the late Al Simmons, was less gracious. "How much do you want to bet that you don't hit .400?" he challenged.

Ted says he answered, "Nuts."

By mid-September Ted's average had risen to .413. Then the weather grew cooler and so did Ted's bat. So the chase ended with Williams at .3995 and only that one Sunday doubleheader in Philadelphia left to play. It had rained on Saturday and was still wet and cold at game time —not Williams' kind of weather.

The night before, manager Joe Cronin had gone to Ted. "Sit it out, Ted, it doesn't mean anything; you have your .400," he said. It was true. Only pedantic historians would note that .3995 has to be rounded off to reach .400.

"No, I don't want it that way," said the perverse perfectionist. "I'll play."

A sportswriter once said, "If Williams were a racehorse, he'd want it to rain each time he got to the starting gate."

To prepare for the twin bill, Ted took his good friend, Johnny Orlando, the clubhouse attendant, on a stroll around the damp streets of Philadelphia. They covered several miles. Ted would wait while Johnny fortified himself at various watering holes.

Next day, when Williams came to bat in the first inning, Frankie Hayes, the Athletics' catcher, said, "Ted, Mr. Mack told us if we let up on you he'll run us out of baseball. I wish you all the luck in the world, but we're not giving you a damn thing."

The umpire was a bit less scrupulous. As Bill McGowan bent over to dust the plate, Williams heard him mutter some advice: "To hit .400 a batter has got to be loose."

Ted was. First he hit a line shot into right field, then a home run, then two more singles. Well above .400 now, he still wouldn't sit down for the second game, banging out two more hits, one a double that broke the loudspeaker horn. Games that meant nothing had suddenly become famous. Not one of a hundred middle-aged baseball fans may remember who won (Boston took both), but a surprising number remember, "Oh yeah, that's the time Williams played at the end of the season when he didn't have to. Got all those hits too."

Will there ever be another .400 hitter? Probably not. The last one to come close was a 39-year-old Red Sox outfielder, who in 1957 missed it by nine or ten hits. A younger hitter would have added enough leg hits to raise the mark well over .400. But first he would have needed the sweet swing of ageless Ted Williams.

Above left: Harry Heilmann, last American Leaguer to hit .400 before Williams, encouraged Ted. *Above right:* batting practice pitcher extraordinaire, Joe Dobson.

Before the Finale

History's success groupies remember 1948 as the year the Cleveland Indians won the only American League playoff and then defeated the National League's Boston Braves in the World Series. They recall player-manager-MVP Lou Boudreau and his surprise pitching choice for that famous playoff game—lefty Gene Beardon, behind whom the Tribe thrashed the Red Sox and Denny Galehouse 8-3. But what of the rest of that year's hectic pennant race, in particular its thrilling final weekend? Those memories are reserved for Red Sox fans and others who have gone to bed at night pennant-hungry, sustained only by the meager fare of unfulfilled fantasy and near triumph.

For their sake at least, this is how the American League contenders stood on Saturday morning, October 3, 1948:

	W.	L.		To Play
Cleveland	95	67		2
Boston	94	68	−1	2
New York	94	68	−1	2

Both Boston and New York were down to their last gasps. Cleveland was playing two games against Detroit at Cleveland. One victory for the Indians would guarantee them a tie; a sweep would clinch the pennant—regardless of how the Red Sox or Yankees fared in their two-game, head-to-head clash at Fenway. As if the situation were not desperate enough for Boston and New York, an embarrassed Steve O'Neill (the Tigers' manager) sent a telegram to both Yankees manager Bucky Harris and the Sox' skipper, Joe McCarthy, with more bad news: "Sorry I can't use intended starter Hutchinson—Fred is in bed with a temperature of 102—but Lou Kretlow will handle Cleveland."

"Who the hell is Lou Kretlow?" moaned both the Yankees and the Red Sox.

It had been a zany race from the beginning. Four teams, the Indians, Yankees, Red Sox, and, until August, Connie Mack's Athletics, had held first place, none more fleetingly than the Red Sox. "They've been writing us off all year," said McCarthy. "They counted us out early when we were eleven games behind in the summer. They counted us out last week." He stopped for a second and smiled. "Well, there are only two games left, and we're still alive."

One of the main reasons for the Red Sox' continuing viability was the man who would pitch against the Yankees this balmy, September Saturday, Jack Kramer. Remembering Jake Ruppert's old strategy, owner Tom Yawkey had sent a Brinks armored car loaded with cash to St. Louis after the disappointing 1947 season and acquired pitcher Kramer and shortstop Vern Stephens. Vern finished the season with 137 RBIs (16 more than Yastrzemski's league-leading total in 1967), and Jack contributed a personal high of 18 victories. The last and most important of them would come today.

Bucky Harris opposed Kramer with Tommy Byrne, a 28-year-old left hander who could be either very good or as wild as a headhunter. In this game he was just wild, passing five in his 2⅓ innings. Three of the walks were harmless enough, but the other two immediately preceded the appearance of Boston's enforcer, number "9." In the opening inning, Williams punished Byrne for walking

Shortstop Vern Stephens forces Yanks' Phil Rizzuto. Boston beat New York this year, but Cleveland was another, sadder story.

Pesky in front of him by blasting one into the right field bullpen. It was a blunt warning never to walk the batter ahead of Williams, but today Byrne was living dangerously. He gave another free ride to Pesky opening the third, then surrendered a double to Williams. Only Joe DiMaggio's fine stop on the play in front of the right center field bleachers stopped Pesky from scoring. After fanning Stephens, Byrne intentionally walked Doerr in favor of the left-handed hitting Stan Spence with a play at any base, but Stan foiled the strategy by singling to right, scoring Pesky. Williams scored on Billy Goodman's fly to Hank Bauer, and the Sox led 4-0. In the fifth Dominic DiMaggio scored from third on Stephens' fly ball to brother Joe, but Kramer made it all quite superfluous. He starved New York's pennant hopes on a total of five hits and only one run.

The word from the shores of Lake Erie was as bleak as the weather there. On a dark, dismal day, dampened by intermittent rain, the Indians exploded for an 8-0 win over Detroit. Knuckleballing Gene Beardon hypnotized the Tigers, and the American League's first black, Larry Doby, went four for four. From the shower Cleveland players serenaded their player-manager, Lou Boudreau, with "One More River to Cross" as he told reporters, "I'll use Feller tomorrow; he's always done well against [Detroit's Hal] Newhouser." (He had won seven of their eight previous meetings.)

McCarthy didn't seem concerned. "I told you we were still alive," he said. "Now if only Newhouser can beat Feller tomorrow."

"One down and one to go," said ace right hander Ellis Kinder. "I hope I can pitch the playoff."

"Let's get there first," cautioned Vern Stephens.

Now that they had knocked the Yankees out of the race, the whole team was sure it could win on Sunday. On Saturday evening, the brothers DiMaggio had dinner in a Boston bistro. The "Yankee Clipper" was visibly upset by the elimination of his ball club. "I'll get even tomorrow," threatened Joe. "You're going to watch [home run] number forty go over that screen."

"Guiseppe, you're all wet this time," replied the "Little Professor." "This year it's our baby. The only DiMaggio home run tomorrow will be my number nine!" Surprisingly enough, Dom was right.

McCarthy started his reliable workhorse, Joe Dobson, and it was Harris' turn to use a surprise starter, rookie Bob Porterfield. Amused Red Sox fans claimed they could hear Lou Boudreau screaming all the way from Cleveland. "What the hell is Harris doing to me; where's Raschi?" Even without their ace, the Yankees were not yet ready to concede the last game. They struck in the opening inning, when Joe D. doubled home Tommy Henrich, and again in the second, when Snuffy Stirnweiss knocked in Bauer. However, a two-run lead at Fenway is about as secure as the Italian government.

Dominic opened Boston's third by singling to right. After Pesky had flied out, Williams beat the shift by slicing one down the left field line. Caught completely by surprise, left fielder Bauer allowed Dom to score. Ted ended up at second. Stephens then beat out an infield hit, and Doerr scored both Ted and Vern with a lusty double to right center.

The capacity crowd soon realized it had more than its Red Sox to scream about. Not only was Boston

116

leading 3-2 with the rally still alive, but the portable radios in the stands were reporting even more favorable news: the Tigers were clobbering Bobby Feller! "Who just doubled, George Kell?"

"I don't know, but Detroit has three."

On the Fenway diamond, Spence walked and Goodman then singled home Doerr. Boston picked up another on a Tebbetts ground out, and Raschi replaced Porterfield. The inning finally ended, and the Red Sox scoreboard operator immediately ignited a new round of delirium by simultaneously hanging up two very important numbers—5 for Boston and 4 for Detroit. The roar was heard across the river in Harvard Yard.

The Yankees cooled the celebration with two runs in the fifth (lefty Ken Johnson replaced Dobson), but the Red Sox revived the party in the sixth. Dom opened the inning with his predicted ninth home run, and Pesky followed with a bunt single that Ty Cobb couldn't have bettered. Raschi fooled Ted—a pop-up—but he grooved one to Stephens, who sent it into the screen. Allie Reynolds replaced Raschi (no one can say Harris gave up), but he brought little improvement. Spence walked and Goodman cracked his third single of the day, scoring Doerr. The Red Sox led 8-4, and from Cleveland came more good news: the Tigers were blasting again.

The Yankees scored again in the seventh, forcing McCarthy to rush in the hero of 1946, Boo Ferriss, but in the bottom of the frame, Williams rebuilt the lead by knocking in Boston's tenth run with his second double of the game. Joe DiMaggio, who had played the game with a charley horse, cracked his fourth hit in the ninth, but with the outcome no longer in doubt, Steve Souchock was sent in to replace him. As the great one left the field, he received a thunderous cheer from the New England fans, always appreciative of class, especially when they are ahead 10-5. Moments later, the race culminated in a flat-footed tie. The Sox had trounced the Yankees; Newhouser had handcuffed Cleveland. The Indians were coming to Fenway for a playoff the next day.

The Red Sox' locker room bubbled like a James Michael Curley election headquarters after a landslide. "They counted us out; they counted us out," McCarthy kept repeating.

Williams turned to veteran Wally Moses. "Who the hell will Boudreau use tomorrow?"

"It has to be [Bob] Lemon, and he's been tough against us all year," Moses answered.

Ted then yelled at the top of his lungs, "I don't care if he's beaten us twenty times this year. We'll knock his brains out tomorrow!"

McCarthy was still chuckling when the reporters, eager to forget that some of them had labeled him a "push-button" manager, crowded around him as if he were a guru. "How about you, Joe? I suppose it has to be Kinder or Parnell."

"Ellie will have had four days' rest," said another, "and Mel three."

"Well," said Joe, "you saw the bullpen today; I had everyone out there." He then scratched his head. "Maybe I'll get the word tonight in a dream. Or better still, just find some nice little man and rub his curly head." There are still those in New England who swear that is what McCarthy must have done. Shortly before game time the next afternoon (author Al Hirshberg says it was only 30 minutes), he walked over to Denny Galehouse and gave him the game ball.

To Recapture the Dream

On August 1, 1972, the Red Sox stood 47-47. They finished the season at 85-70, a half game out of first place. Thus, a good Boston team got hot, winning almost two-thirds of its last 60 games, but once again missed out and spent the winter dreaming of the never-never land of might-have-been.

In 1971, the Red Sox finished in third place, 18 games behind the Orioles. Such a finish always evokes trading fever in general manager Dick O'Connell. So off to Milwaukee went George Scott, Ken Brett, and Jim Lonborg for Tommy Harper and Marty Pattin. (There were others involved, but these five were the key.) Scott's departure left a hole at first base: enter Danny Cater from New York; exit bullpen stalwart Albert ("Sparky") Lyle. He left with a blunt farewell: "I don't really feel I'm wanted around here anymore."

The Milwaukee trade earned the headlines; the Lyle trade lost the pennant and perhaps more. Then came the players' strike, which, when finally settled, cost Boston seven games and Detroit, the chief competition-to-be, only six. As only a half game separated the two clubs at the finish, the one more game that Boston missed might have been the difference. Thus, before the season had even begun, the Lyle trade and the players' strike had molded, if not fully determined, Boston's fate.

On April 19, just days after the foreshortened season had begun, another event greatly (but this time favorably) influenced the Red Sox' fortunes. On that day (while Lyle saved the first of 35 games for the Yankees), the Indians stole four bases on Boston catcher Bob Mont- gomery, prompting manager Eddie Kasko to replace him with rookie Carlton Fisk. "Fisk may be inexperienced," said Kasko, "but at least he can throw." He could hit, too. The young man would hit .293 for the year with 22 home runs and 61 RBIs, and would win the Rookie of the Year award by a unanimous vote.

As he made the decision on the nineteenth to go with the rookie who would develop into a firebrand behind the plate, Kasko also saw an indication of his future leader of the pitching corps. Luis Tiant would take somewhat longer than Fisk to come to the fore, but when he struck out four in two innings of relief on the nineteenth, he presaged an August and September skein of 11 victories in 13 games that would earn him the Comeback Player of the Year award.

Fisk and Tiant were the most pleasant surprises for the Red Sox in their surge that fell short, but there were other vital factors as well.

118

Opposite: In 1972 again, Yaz was hot in the stretch. Here he yells in triumph after socking two-run game-winning homer in Baltimore. *Above:* Tigers' Dick McAuliffe scores game and pennant winner October **3**.

Marty Pattin floundered at 2-8 with an ERA of 5.67, then reversed himself, pitched magnificently in the stretch, and finished at 17-13. Finally finding his power after an early-season injury and slump, Yaz contributed 8 of his 12 home runs in September.

On the morning of September 26, the Red Sox stood atop the East Division by one game. Only Detroit remained to challenge Boston. "We've got to look out for those three games at Baltimore and the final three at Tiger Stadium," warned super-scout Frank Malzone after the Sox split with the Tigers at Fenway and prepared for the final week.

When it was over, one Boston writer lamented, "They did great in August and September; if only they had won one more in October."

September 26

Two-run homers by both Yaz and Pattin gave Boston an early 4-0 lead over the Brewers. It might have been more: with the bases loaded and two outs in the fifth, Ollie Brown flashed across the outfield to rob Fisk of a seemingly sure triple. Then in the eighth, leading by only 4-2 now, Boston fell apart. Brock Davis opened with a bunt that handcuffed Rico Petrocelli at third. With one out, Davis stole second and continued to third when Aparicio and second baseman Doug Griffin couldn't decide who would cover the base and allowed Fisk's throw to sail into center. Ellie Rodriguez sent Davis home with a fly to center, cutting the lead to 4-3. Then Joe Lahoud reached first when Yastrzemski fielded his ground ball but couldn't get it out of the glove, and George ("Boomer") Scott avenged the slur of having been traded by belting one into the center field bleachers—quite a clout at Fenway. Afterward, the exultant Scott said, "If I tell you I'm not fired up coming in here, I'm telling a lie."

The Red Sox had blown one, and their lead over the idle Tigers had shrunk to a half game.

September 27

Former Bostonian Ken Brett failed where fellow alumnus Scott had succeeded the day before. Boston raked Milwaukee 7-5, thanks mainly to Aparicio's two singles and triple and Bill ("Spaceman") Lee's relief work.

The Tigers kept pace by turning an eighth-inning 5-1 deficit into a 6-5 win at Tiger Stadium over New York's Sparky Lyle, a Boston nemesis even in defeat.

September 28

Kansas City stopped in Boston for a makeup game. It would be the last game of the year at Fenway. John Curtis pitched well enough for a shutout but was satisfied with a 3-1 win. The deciding runs scored on Griffin's single and a wild pitch.

Solo homers by Thurman Munson and, of all people, reliever Lindy McDaniel took the Yankees to the twelfth inning against Mickey Lolich at Detroit. Then Roy White won it for New York with the Yankees' third circuit clout.

Only six more to go: three in Baltimore and then three in the Tigers' den. The Sox left for the last road trip at 82-67, a not invincible but seemingly secure game and a half ahead of Detroit (81-69).

September 29

Luis Tiant, hero of 1972, won his eleventh game since August 1 when Yaz, hero of 1967, homered in the tenth. Orioles manager Earl Weaver went to the mound in the tenth to ask his pitcher, Jim Palmer, "Do you want to walk him?"

"No, I'll pitch him high and outside," the pitcher responded. Yaz went with the pitch.

Another hero of 1967 found his championship form more elusive this day. The Tigers clobbered Jim Lonborg and the Brewers at Detroit 12-5.

September 30

Marty Pattin, saved by Veale, provided the pitching and Yaz another rerun of 1967. Carl began by singling home Tommy Harper in the second. In the eighth, with a two and two count, he checked his swing, according to umpire Jim Odom. The ruling brought Weaver vituperating from the dugout, for which protest Odom dismissed the manager for the evening. It proved a prudent decision for Weaver might have become a menace after the next pitch, which Carl knocked into the bleachers.

Pattin took a 3-1 lead into the ninth, but he was obviously tiring. Brooks Robinson began the frame with a single. When Pattin walked Bobby Grich, who had struck out in his three previous times at bat, manager Eddie Kasko called for the 6-foot 5-inch, left-handed Veale. With a strikeout, Bob aborted Johnny Oates's attempt to move the runners along. Then he slipped a third strike past Dave Johnson, batting for Mark Belanger. When Al Bumbry, running for Robinson, took off for third on the strikeout pitch, Fisk recovered from his surprise and heaved a perfect throw to Rico to nip the fleet-footed Bumbry for the last out of the game.

In the Motor City the impeccable Al Kaline rapped out four hits, including a home run, as the Tigers devastated Milwaukee 13-4, Joe Coleman's nineteenth win of the year. With understated prescience Al remarked, "Let's hope I can keep it up for the next four games."

October 1

Ageless Mike Cuellar will never pitch another game in which so many well-hit balls do so little damage. The height of the frustration for Boston came in the fourth, when trailing 1-0, the Red Sox bunched three of their eight hits off Mike without scoring. Luis Aparicio opened with a clothesline single to center. After Yaz flied out, Reggie Smith beat out a cheapie, a check-swing single to second. Rico followed with a hard shot into the hole on the left side. If it had gone through, Luis might have scored, but it didn't—the shortstop knocked it down. With the bases loaded now, Fisk popped up, leaving it up to the rookie, Dwight Evans. The 20-year-old smashed one to the left of Brooks Robinson. "I never could imagine that it wasn't a hit—I drilled it," Evans said later. But the peerless Brooks reached the ball with his patented lunge, straightened, and threw to second to force Rico.

In the sixth the line drive syndrome continued. With two outs, Reggie singled, Rico walked, and Carlton Fisk lined a single to center, scoring Smith and tying the score at 1-1. But then the Sox were deprived of more when Griffin's bullet flew directly at the left fielder.

After Bobby Grich hit a low inside fastball out in the Orioles' sixth, the Red Sox missed still another beautiful opportunity in the top of the ninth. With one out, Evans singled to center and Griffin to right. Kasko sent up Bob Montgomery to hit for Bill Lee, who had replaced McGlothen. Monty ran the count to 3-2, then slashed a ground ball right at the shortstop—a perfect double play.

In the meantime Aurelio Rodriguez's three-run homer and solo shots by Dick McAuliffe and Al (still hitting) Kaline gave Detroit a comfortable 5-1 victory over Milwaukee. Detroit skipper Billy Martin gambled and won by starting John Hiller, usually a reliever, who won his first game since returning to baseball after a near-fatal heart attack in January 1971. Almost as important as the win itself, Hiller's start allowed Martin to save Lolich for the first game against Boston.

October 2

The best of three for the pennant. Because the Red Sox would play one fewer game than the Tigers, Boston's half-game lead now meant nothing. One team would have to win two of the last three for the title. Boston had won only one of six games in Detroit in 1972, and the winning pitcher in that one, McGlothen, had worked the previous day at Baltimore. "I'll go with Curtis, Luis, and Pattin," said Kasko. "I wish we had them in Boston."

"Thank heavens we have them in Detroit, not Boston," said Martin. "We leave Thursday at five P.M. for Oakland."

Before 52,000 fans, John Curtis faced the potbellied hero of the '68 World Series, Mickey Lolich, whom, it is said, you beat early or not at all. The conventional wisdom would never be truer than this evening.

In his inexorable quest to slug the Tigers into the playoffs, Kaline put Detroit ahead 1-0 in the second with a clout over the left field wall. Boston answered in the third. Curtis opened by striking out, but Harper and Aparicio both singled to left. Yastrzemski then belted one to the deepest part of center field, over the head of the fleet-footed Mickey Stanley. Harper scored easily, but Aparicio, usually one of the best base runners, stumbled as he neared third, regained his balance, rounded third, and fell flat on his face. Instead of scoring, he returned to third, where he met Yaz himself, running all the way on what should have been a triple and perhaps an inside-the-park homer. Unfortunately, bases have room for only one. Yaz was tagged out, and Reggie Smith confirmed the debacle by striking out.

Yaz has said, "We lost it right there; we had Mickey on the ropes and we let him bounce back."

In the fifth Rodriguez broke the tie with a homer. He knocked in two more runs later, icing the 4-1 victory. Having dropped two in a row, the Red Sox now had to win two straight. At least they kept no one in suspense.

October 3

Luis Tiant did not pitch a bad game; Woody Fryman just pitched a better one. He stranded Red Sox on base in the first, fourth, fifth, sixth, and eighth. In the sixth Yaz lined out; in the eighth Aurelio Rodriguez made a spectacular stop on Carlton Fisk's smash. But for the most part, Tom Yawkey's postmortem was as accurate as it was succinct. "We had a good team—I liked our pitching," the owner said. "We just stopped hitting." Thus, led by Fryman, who was 10-3 after joining the Tigers in August, and Kaline, who went 22 for 44 down the stretch, Detroit won 3-1 and took the division by a half game over Boston. (The Sox won the final game in Detroit.)

Perhaps it would have been different had Boston kept Lyle or had the players' strike not deprived the Red Sox of one more game than it did the Tigers. It would certainly have been different had the Red Sox done better than 33-44 on the road, particularly in Motown, where they were 2-7. Whatever the reasons, instead of winning they merely came close, and reminded those who may have been too young to recall 1948 and 1949 that the pennant race legacy of the Red Sox includes heartbreak as well as Impossible Dreams come true.

MANAGERS

William ("Rough") Carrigan

"He was the greatest manager I ever played for."

—Babe Ruth

The same praise comes from Larry Gardner, Carl Mays, and any number of the Red Sox who played during the years 1913-16. It would be extremely difficult to improve on Carrigan's three full years at the helm in the mid-teens. Taking over from Jake Stahl in the summer of 1913, he immediately began building the team that was to win two world championships. The next year he brought the Red Sox into second place and in 1915 and 1916 went all the way.

After starring at Holy Cross both as a football halfback and catcher,

Rough Carrigan was perhaps the Red Sox' greatest manager. He guided Boston to two flags in his first three and a half years.

Rough joined the Red Sox in 1906. Never a strong hitter (.257 lifetime), he was one of the great defensive catchers of his day. Jack Barry, who replaced him as manager, called him the greatest guardian of home plate in the business. "Could he guard that plate; he'd even sit on it if he had to. I've seen men much bigger than Rough crash into him and Bill would be the one standing."

"He brought me up and taught me how to be a big league pitcher," said Babe Ruth. "He knew all the hitters in the league and how to pitch to them. Nobody waved off Rough's signs."

His teams of 1915 and 1916 made those years two of the brightest in Red Sox history. Using the great outfield of Lewis, Hooper, and Speaker as his base, he forged a unit that finished ahead of the Tigers of Cobb, Crawford, Heilmann, and Veach and also defeated the Phillies in a five-game World Series. After losing the first game to the sensational Pete Alexander, the Sox swept the next four.

This was the Series when after each game Ruth went to Carrigan and inquired, "Am I going to work tomorrow, Rough?"

"No, Babe," answered Carrigan, and he always had a reason. Ruth had won 18 games that year and desperately wanted to work in the Series. He never did. It's hard to understand it all, but it's equally hard to argue with a manager who wins a five-game World Series.

In 1916, Carrigan needed all his managerial skills. Owner Joe Lannin and Tris Speaker were at each others' throats. Lannin felt that Speaker had held him up for more money, threatening to jump to the Federal League. Well, the Feds were deader than a mackerel on a Provincetown pier, but the sensibilities of the two combatants demanded a decision on the merits. Lannin's was moronic; he peddled Tris to Cleveland on the eve of the season's opener. Carrigan found himself about to defend his world championship without his star center fielder.

Rough called a clubhouse meeting. "All right, so Joe has sold the cowboy, but we can still win without him. There's no better pitching staff in baseball and that's what wins pennants." Carrigan was right. He did have the best staff in the game, and no one could direct them any better than he could.

Ruth led the pack by piling up 23 wins and a league-leading ERA of 1.75. No American League left hander has been lower since. Carl Mays won 19, Dutch Leonard 18, Ernie Shore 15, and Rube Foster 14. Both Foster and Leonard treated the fans of Fenway to no-hitters that year, Rube against the Yankees and Dutch over St. Louis.

While he was still a playing manager, Bill rarely went behind the plate. Most of his time was spent watching over his hurlers like a mother hen. Larry Gardner spoke with the certainty of age when he said, "In all my years in baseball, I never knew anyone who could work with the battery any better than Bill. He seemed to have an uncanny knowledge of just how long to go with a pitcher."

It was fortunate that the pitching was great because the Sox of 1916 would have never won it on hitting. Only Gardner hit over .300 (.308). The rest of the team, including Hooper and Lewis, had off years at the plate. The team average dropped 12 points from .260 to .248. For an entire team 12 points is a lot of base hits. The Tigers, on the other hand, hit .264 and together with the White Sox pushed Carrigan's men right to the finish. But Boston prevailed and ravaged Uncle Wilbert Robinson's Brooklyn team in the World Series.

Now it was Rough's turn to startle the baseball world. "I'm going to retire," announced Bill. "I have business affairs down in Maine [banks and a theater chain] that demand my attention." He was offered large additional sums of money to stay, but the best they could get from him was, "If the team ever really needs me, I'll come back."

It's too bad he did. In 1927, he finally succumbed to the urgings and returned as manager. It was to prove the greatest mistake of his life. The team he inherited had developed an addiction to last place, one not to be broken until the entrance of Yawkey in 1933.

At first the writers were delighted with Carrigan's return. "Watch what happens now; Bill will turn them around," was the message from the scribes all over New England. However, an outfield of Skinny Shaner (who?), Ira Flagstead, and John Tobin was not the Golden Outfield; Slim Harris was not Babe Ruth. In short the team stank. Bill tried it for three disastrous years, decided it was hopeless, and threw in the towel. His sole accomplishment from 1926 to 1928 was proving the time-honored axiom, "You can't win 'em without the players".

Carrigan's second tenure as manager has been mercifully forgotten by all but the record books. Fortunately the first has not been. Bill remains the only manager in Red Sox history to win two consecutive World Series. As a developer of pitchers, he still stands peerless at Fenway, perhaps in baseball.

Joe Cronin

Joe Cronin began as a weak-hitting utility infielder and wound up the president of the American League. On the way up he won a Most Valuable Player award (in 1930), twice led the league in doubles and once in triples, and established a career batting average of .301. With

all due respect to Luke Appling and Arky Vaughan, one must rate him the premier shortstop of the thirties. In 1956, during his controversial and less than successful career as a general manager, his prowess as a player was saluted when he was elected to the Hall of Fame.

As a manager, Cronin was not a rousing success, but neither was he a failure. After winning the pennant as the player-manager of the Senators in 1933, he moved to the Red Sox for the 1935 season, succeeding Bucky Harris. Vice-president Eddie Collins told him, "We'll get you the players; you work with them." Unfortunately, some of them were not easy to work with. Cronin

had to deal with such characters as Billy Werber, Ben Chapman, Lefty Grove, Wes Ferrell, Bobo Newsom, and Jim Tabor—a crew that might have provided an interesting case study for a psychologist but not a pennant for even the most understanding manager. Once Cronin instructed Chapman to move along a runner with a bunt. The outfielder went to the plate, promptly swung away, and hit into a double play. When reminded later that he had ignored his manager's orders, Chapman faced Cronin and snarled, "I don't sacrifice."

Selfishness was not the only reason that Cronin's club did not win in the late thirties. Another was the New York Yankees, who were rated by no less an authority than Frank Graham as almost as good as the Murderers' Row teams of 1927 and 1928. Still another handicap was the lack of a real stopper on the pitching staff. On the team that finished second in 1938, nine games out, no pitcher won more than 15 games.

During the war years of 1943-45, Cronin, like the rest of the managers, had to try to fashion a big league team with a potpourri of 4F's, ancients, and children. The talent crunch forced Cronin to remain a playing manager long after he would have been content to direct the team from the bench, but playing past his prime had its triumphant moments. "I guess the old man showed them today," he remarked gleefully after he had won both games of a doubleheader with pinch-hit homers against the Athletics on June 17, 1943. During the season of 1943, he hit five pinch-hit homers, establishing a record.

When one of Cronin's teams finally did finish in first place, in 1946, it seemed as if a new Red

126

Above: Joe Cronin with a crosstown rival, Casey Stengel, manager of the Boston Bees. *Opposite:* players hoist Cronin after 1946 pennant clincher. Left to right: Johnny Pesky, Cronin, Tom McBride, Earl Johnson.

Sox dynasty was at hand. But his two pitching heroes of 1946, Tex Hughson and Boo Ferriss, fell apart the next year, Cronin's last at the helm.

In 1948, the Red Sox jumped at the opportunity to sign Joe McCarthy as manager and elevated Cronin to vice-president/general manager, which ended his 13-season stint as field manager, the longest by far in Sox history. Other than the war years, 1936 was his only losing year.

Because the main function of a general manager is to build a winner, Cronin's rating as a Red Sox executive must be low. The 1948-50 teams, acquired mainly while Collins was still in charge, were the only contenders during Cronin's 11 years as boss. Critics charged "cronyism," picturing Joe as a fat politician whose greatest concern was to take care of his friends. One writer observed, "I don't think a single scout was fired when Cronin was GM. Some of them were friends that went back to his days with the Pirates."

There were good points too, however. Jimmy Piersall, Jackie Jensen, Sammy White, Bill Monbouquette, and Frank Malzone all joined the club under Cronin, and the surprising team of 1955 (only two games out in August) could have done it all with a strong starting pitcher to supplement one of Cronin's better acquisitions, Frank Sullivan.

The most damaging problem during the Cronin stewardship was the Red Sox' inability to develop black players. Whether, as rumors have it, they could have had any or all of the great ones, starting with Satch Paige, the fact remains that Boston's first black player arrived some 12 years after Jackie Robinson broke the color barrier. And Pumpsie Green was hardly worth waiting for. The author is not suggesting that Cronin purposely excluded blacks. During the race of 1955, Cronin probably would have asked Yawkey to mortgage Fenway if he thought that would induce the Cubs to part with Ernie Banks, a shortstop who would have had little difficulty displacing the Red Sox' best at the time, Billy Klaus.

In 1959, Cronin terminated a 24-year association with the Red Sox by becoming president of the American League. His career at Boston had been paradoxical—as he moved into positions of greater responsibility, he did worse: an excellent player, a good manager, a mediocre general manager.

Dick Williams

To understand Dick Williams, remember what he did after Tom Yawkey fired him in 1970. He had one year left on his contract with Boston and thus could have sat out the 1970 season at full pay. But not one to live off the fat of the land, Williams went to Montreal to coach under Gene Mauch. A year later he was in Oakland under tempestuous Charley Finley—a brilliant if short-lived marriage of convenience between an ambitious but independent manager and an equally ambitious but dictatorial owner. Before the marriage collapsed, Williams had produced three division titles and two World Series triumphs in three years. Thus, after sliding from idolization to infamy in four short years with Boston, he promptly reversed the procedure and in another four years became the most acclaimed manager in baseball once again.

He has made a career of bouncing back. After a shoulder injury in 1953 cost him his job as a player with the Dodgers, he came back to the majors in 1956 with Baltimore and lasted until 1964. In 1960, at Kansas City, he batted .288 in 130 games as both an infielder and outfielder and led the team in RBIs with 75.

He began in managing by guiding Boston's Triple A team in the International League, Toronto, to playoff victories in 1965 and 1966. Then he moved to the big club and transformed it from a league-leading loser to a pennant winner, the only time an American League team has led the league in losses one year and in wins the next.

Now Williams is at the helm of the last-place California Angels and

determined to become the second manager in history to win pennants with three different clubs.

You won the International League playoffs those two years in Toronto. Who were some of the players you had at Toronto who helped win in sixty-seven at Boston?

Well, there was Reggie Smith, Joe Foy, Mike Andrews, and Russ Gibson. Then there was Gary Waslewski. Gary did a tremendous job for me at Toronto—won more

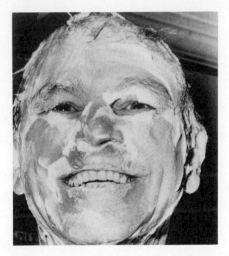

games than anybody in the league. I always thought he would make it in the majors, but he never really did.

What about Reggie Smith? He never seemed to reach his real potential at Boston.

Well, I don't know, he played well for me in sixty-seven, sixty-eight, and sixty-nine. He was an improving ball player with me each year I had him. He led the league in sixty-six at Toronto—then he played well as a kid under all that pressure in sixty-seven. The man's a super athlete, really super. I'm really not in a position to say what happened after I left, but I wish I had him now. Boston traded him [to St. Louis for pitcher Rick Wise] in one of those moves that is supposed to help both teams. Maybe it still will. You really can't anticipate a pitcher getting arm trouble. The Red Sox needed pitching help and you have to give up something to get something.

It has been said that you really laid down the law when you took over the Sox. Has this strictness of yours been exaggerated?

Probably not. I had to be stern, real firm. Remember, I'd been there as a player just a couple of years before [1963 and 1964]. The talent was there, no doubt about it—it was my job to bring it out. We put in bed checks, the whole thing. It was a point of getting back to fundamentals, on the field and off. I guess you might say I was as firm as you can be. A few of the players ob-

Opposite: foamy victory in 1967. *Left and above:* two of Williams' young charges on the 1967 team who left Boston shortly after he did—George Scott and Reggie Smith.

129

jected, some pretty strenuously, but I noticed they picked up their World Series checks at the end of the year.

Care to comment about your two years as a Red Sox player?

Most of my two years was spent as a pinch hitter or as Dick Stuart's caddy. Whenever Stuart was on a team, you had constant chaos. He's the only guy I ever knew that was given a standing ovation by the fans for catching a piece of paper that was blowing on the field. You can't win a pennant with guys like Stuart.

I did have a good pinch-hitting record one year there [16 for 48 or .333 in 1963]. I can also remember hitting some home runs. In sixty-four I was only up about sixty times, but five of my eleven hits were home runs—three of them in a row. There was one time when I hit back to back home runs with Tony Conigliaro to beat the Yankees. But those teams were bad. Actually, they had some good players, but they couldn't play together as a unit.

One of the first things you did in sixty-seven was eliminate the captain's job. Why?

I had nothing against having a captain. I had Sal Bando and then in L.A. Frank Robinson. It's a nice honorary title, but it depends on the circumstances. Yaz didn't want to be captain anyway, so I made one simple statement: "We'll have only one chief, all the rest are Indians." We had no friction on that. Look at the year he [Yastrzemski] had—he was the natural leader anyway. I wanted to shake them up; they hadn't been going anywhere—a perennial second-division ball club.

You picked up a team in sixty-seven that had finished ninth the year before. Surely you didn't feel at the beginning that you could win it. When then did it first dawn on you that Boston could go all the way?

No, not at the beginning. The only statement I made was, "We'll win more than we'll lose." It was just a matter of execution. That game that Lonborg won against Detroit just before the All-Star break was certainly one of the turning points. He was in trouble all the time but got out of it. We'd lost several games just before that. This was the one that turned us around. We went on a ten-game winning streak—plus one in Baltimore where we were ahead, with Waslewski pitching. But the rain came before the fifth inning. After that I think everyone on the team felt that we could do it.

You received a lot of publicity about [Joe] Foy and [George] Scott in sixty-seven and their weight problems. What about it?

Scott, more than Foy. I was very strict with him about keeping his weight down. We had a series in Anaheim with a day off before it started. Scott showed up seven pounds over—I don't know how he did it in one day. Anyway, I didn't play him the whole series—oh, I guess he pinch hit once—but I had to be firm. We lost all three games, incidentally, but if you give in one place, you're lost. [Jim] Fregosi said, "We have nine managers in the league and one dietician."

When it was all over, I said, "Well, the dietician won!"

Did Elston Howard contribute

much during those last two months?

Yes. He certainly did, a *great* deal. He didn't hit much, but we didn't get him for his bat. He contributed quite a bit, both behind the plate and just talking to our pitchers. We really didn't have any pitchers who'd been in a close race; Ellie knew all about it.

What about the Maglie incident? [Pitching coach Sal Maglie was abruptly dismissed after the 1967 season. He had been a Sox coach since 1965.]

A hell of a pitcher. I saw plenty of him in the National League. But I don't think too much of him as a pitching coach. He had one year to go on his contract, so there was nothing I could do in sixty-seven. I replaced him as soon as I could. Maglie didn't care much for the way it was done, but I didn't hire him, so I didn't fire him. I let [general manager] Dick O'Connell do that.

Can you say something about the crowds in sixty-seven at Fenway?

In sixty-seven we didn't draw at the beginning. Then we started our thing and they were buying tickets right into the finish. I remember—I think it was in July—we'd just been beaten in a ball game by the Twins. I said this race will probably go right down to those last two games with Minnesota. Someone, I think it was Larry Claflin, wrote it up. The race was just forming with the four clubs and the crowds really started coming in. It seemed every game was capacity; that old park was really humming. We ended up double the previous year in attendance [1,727,832] and in sixty-eight we almost drew two million in a park that seats thirty-three thousand.

What do you feel was the best trade engineered while you were manager of the Red Sox?

Those two deals when we acquired Gary Bell and Jerry Adair within a week in early June of sixty-seven. Shortly after we got Adair, Rico broke his wrist and was out for four weeks. Adair filled in great. Then, when Andrews was hurt, he moved over to second. Bell won twelve games after he came over and only lost a couple. Then there was the Harrelson acquisition. Ken didn't do too much in sixty-seven—although I'll never forget a run he knocked in with a ground ball the last game of the season—but what a year he had in sixty-eight. Led the league in RBIs. Ken had real power.

After the great year of sixty-seven, you ended up seventeen games out in sixty-eight. What happened?

It had to be Lonborg and that damn skiing. [Lonborg tore ligaments in his knee while skiing at Lake Tahoe during the off-season and missed much of the year. He won only six games.] But don't forget Santiago. He started off great for us in sixty-eight. As a matter of fact, I picked him for the All-Star Game. When he went on the disabled list [July 19], we were through. Of course, George Scott's falling apart didn't help any.

You know, losing Lonborg and Santiago really influenced my last two years at Boston. From then on we were always looking for pitchers. Dick Ellsworth and Ray Culp were two we got. Dick won sixteen games for us in sixty-eight and Culp was great in both sixty-eight and sixty-nine. I would never have given up Ken Harrelson if we weren't so much in need of pitching. Sonny Siebert and Vincente Romo were the key for me in that trade. Romo was a disappointment, but Sonny pitched some great ball. He was also quite a hitter himself.

Can you say anything about leaving the Red Sox?

I didn't hit it off with Mr. Yawkey. That was the main reason. He said, "Williams has a communication gap with the players." I don't know, maybe I stepped on a few toes. Maybe Yawkey thought I was too tough or too cruel on the players.

You didn't have any run-ins with him, did you?

Oh, I had a few meetings with him that were pretty rough.

You were certainly pretty close after sixty-seven.

Well, he hadn't won a pennant in twenty-one years; he was a pretty happy guy.

123456789

PLAYERS

Larry Gardner

Larry Gardner has a lot to remember, and he does it with uncanny accuracy. Though he is now 88 years old, he can recall plays of more than 50 years ago as if he had just seen them happen. A visitor who expects a less alert type is no sooner startled with Gardner's lucidity than he is disabused of some other prejudices toward old-timers as well. The ball players of Gardner's day were not, Gardner contends, all the uneducated boors later generations have made them out to be. Many of them were college graduates, which at that time bespoke something of an education. Among the Red Sox, Gardner, Bill Carrigan, Ray Collins, Jack Barry, Harry Hooper, and Duffy Lewis were college men. There certainly were clods, as there are today, but they did not predominate, Gardner says.

Gardner joined the Red Sox in 1908, and soon established himself as their regular third baseman. In 1912, he batted .315 (second on the team only to Tris Speaker), hit the Red Sox' only home run in the World Series, and also knocked in the winning run in the final game. During the 1916 season, he was Boston's leading hitter (.308), and against the Dodgers in the World Series, he hit two home runs, one a game winner.

Gardner moved to Philadelphia in 1918 and to Cleveland the next year. There he played on the World Series winner of 1920 (under manager and former teammate Speaker). He played in the game against the Yankees in August of that year when Carl Mays mortally wounded Ray Chapman of the Cleveland Indians with a pitch that struck him on the head.

After his distinguished major league career (.289 lifetime batting average; 1,931 total hits), Gardner managed in the minors and coached at Cleveland. He left professional ball to become coach of the University of Vermont, where he often matched baseball wits with another Red Sox alumnus, Jack Barry, who coached Holy Cross. Gardner now lives directly across from the campus and works part time in a Burlington photo shop.

Mr. Gardner, you first went to the Red Sox in 1908. How did that all come about?

I was playing in the Maine State League and was going great guns. [Red Sox manager] Fred Lake heard about me and sent a scout up to look me over. He signed me on the spot for four hundred dollars a month, just during the season. I left the Maine League with them promising to send me the eighty-five dollars they owed me. The mails must be real slow; I haven't received it yet.

Cy Young was on your first Red Sox team. Can you remember anything about Cy?

Let me tell you about Cy. One of the first games I played in, maybe the first, was against the old New York Highlanders. They had that guy who could "hit 'em where they ain't"—you remember, Willie Keeler. He knew I was a green country boy, and he bunted me to death. And could he bunt! I was very discouraged, thought they were going to send me home, really down in the mouth. Cy came over and said, "Come on, Larry, let's go have a couple."

A funny thing, a lot of people thought Cy didn't drink, but that's

Larry Gardner slides home safely on his three-run, inside-the-park homer against Dodgers in the fourth game of 1916 Series.

crazy. Cy drank plenty but never a night before a game he was going to pitch. We went over to the Hotel Putnam on Huntington Avenue. That's where most of the players used to go in those days. Cy ordered some rye whiskey called Cascade— how he loved that Cascade. Don't see it anymore. Then he told me not to worry, everyone's nervous at first; I'd be all right. Well, that sure picked me up. Imagine drinking whiskey with Cy Young and being told you were going to make it! He was quite a guy!

Speaking of bunting, did Cobb "bunt you to death"?

He sure didn't. I found out Ty's secret early and never told him. I don't think he ever got a bunt hit on me. You see, Ty used to fake a

lot of bunts. But when he was going to really bunt, he'd always lock his lips. When I saw that, I'd start in with the pitch. He never realized I'd caught on.

You played against Cobb all your seventeen years in the American League. What kind of a guy was he?

Ty and I were great friends right up until he died. It went back to my first full season with the Red Sox. Amby McConnell, the second baseman, had an appendicitis attack, and they told me I'd be playing second the next day. I'd never played second in my life. I went out the next morning at ten o'clock and practiced all morning, but I still didn't know all the moves.

We were playing Detroit. Cobb got on first and headed for second. I

Walter Johnson, who lost both games of a doubleheader to the Red Sox in 1916. Gardner knocked in the winning run off Johnson in both.

You mentioned Heinie Wagner. You were teammates for several years. What kind of a guy was Heinie?

Oh, he was a gutsy little guy—real small, but tough as can be. They used to knock him all over, but he wouldn't give an inch. His body was covered with bruises and cuts all season. Heinie didn't hit too well, but he got them when we needed them.

What about the famous Snodgrass muff? Do you remember it?

Like it was yesterday. The Giants had scored in the top of the tenth. We knew we had to score. I remember hearing someone say—I think it was Jake Stahl—"Let's get those lousy bastards!"

Clyde Engle went up to pinch hit. He hit a lazy fly to center. I can see it right now. It just seemed to drop out of his glove. That'll happen to a player every now and then. It sure happened to me. You never realize why you miss it, but you still do.

Then you knocked in the winning run with the sacrifice fly? Do you remember that?

I sure do! I just wanted to get it to the outfield. When I first hit it, I thought it was going out. Then I saw Josh Devore catch it near the fence and I was disappointed for a second. Then I saw Steve [Yerkes] scoring the run and I realized it was over. It meant four thousand twenty-four dollars and sixty-eight cents to me, which just about doubled my earnings for the year.

We didn't make much in those days. I remember that when Yerkes would get paid (we were paid on the fifteenth and thirtieth of the month), he'd run down to the bank and deposit it. Then he'd try to bum

caught the throw and was standing right in his way. If he'd slid into me, he would have cut me up badly. But he tried to slide around me and I tagged him out. When he was walking off, he said to Heinie [Wagner, the Red Sox' shortstop], "Tell the kid I won't give him a break like that again. I would have cut him in two!"

I spent a lot of time defending Ty to people. He was all right with me.

Did you get spiked much in those days? [The old gentleman lifted up his pant legs revealing legs that looked like a road map.]

See that big one at the kneecap? I got that one from George Stone of the Browns. But I put Stone out and we won the game.

136

dollars from the rest of us until pay day. Steven was very penurious.

You also played for Patsy Donovan when he managed. Do you remember Patsy?

Oh, he was a character—very, very religious. Whenever the boys would use profanity on the bench, which was quite often, Patsy would just shake his head and go, "Tish, tish," or "Tut, tut, boys, boys, please don't say those words." He'd been in baseball for thirty years, but he never changed.

While you were with the Red Sox, who were the toughest pitchers for you to hit?

Well, first there was Eddie Plank. All the years I faced him, I only got two hits—a single between short and third and a triple to right. Then there were Red Faber and Ed Walsh. They had tremendous spitballs. You could never tell what the ball was going to do. I know the slider they have today must be very hard to hit, but we had the spitter, the emory ball, the shine ball, all those trick pitches. They were murder!

What about Walter Johnson?

We played a doubleheader with Washington, I think it was in 1916. I knocked in the winning run in the first game when we beat Walter. He came into the second game in the eighth inning—the score was tied. I knocked in the winning run in that one, too, and we won again three to two. Imagine that, beating Johnson twice in the same day!

I figured out Walter early. He was so fast I knew I could never get around on him. I always used a specially made bat, very thick. With Walter I figured that all I had to do was meet the pitch. That's what I

did and it worked very well. Incidentally, Walter was one of the nicest men who ever lived.

What kind of a manager was Bill Carrigan?

Well, Bill and I had been teammates for several years before he became manager. We used to pal around a lot, especially on the road. I don't think anyone was better at blocking the plate than Bill. Boy, was he tough!

I remember one time when we were playing Detroit. George Moriarty was their third baseman. He and Bill were actually good friends. Moriarty got on first and yelled to Bill. "Hey, you Irish SOB," (the funny thing was Moriarty was Irish, too), "I'm going to come around the bases and knock you on your arse." Well, sure enough, George made his way around and came tearing into the plate. It was Moriarty, not Bill, that was knocked over. Bill walked over to George and let go with a hunk of tobacco juice. "And how do you like that, you Irish SOB?"

Bill didn't have a great arm, but he was the smartest catcher I ever saw. He always seemed to know when the runner was going to go. Then he'd throw it out to Heinie on the bounce, and they'd frequently get the runner.

I remember one time after Bill had become manager, one of our hitters had two strikes and no balls. Bill said, "I've got a hunch." He went in as a pinch hitter. I'll be damned if he didn't work the pitcher for a walk.

There was never anything said at the time, but we all knew that Bill had a share in the gate receipts. After each game he'd go up to the office and check them. They weren't going to put anything over on Bill.

To get back to your question, he was the best manager I played for. Tris [Speaker, manager when Larry played for the Indians] was good, also, but Bill was tops.

The outfield of Duffy Lewis, Harry Hooper, and Speaker has frequently been called the greatest ever. Do you agree?

It was the best I ever saw. Of course, everyone remembers how good Tris was. He could play way in and go back with the sound of the bat. He went everywhere. They don't seem to remember how great Harry was—probably just as good—and what an arm! I remember a game against Detroit. There was a runner on third. Someone—I think it was Donie Bush—hit a short fly to right. Harry came tearing in and dove on his belly for the ball. He caught it, rolled over, and came up throwing. I'll be damned if he didn't get the runner at the plate. I never saw anything else like it.

We used to call that little incline in left field Duffy's Cliff. Lewis could really play that wall! It was great to play with that outfield!

Can you remember when the Babe came up?

Yes, I surely can. He was a great big happy kid; he used to smoke as many cigars as I did. But you know, we never would see him much other than at the ball park. He loved the girls and they seemed to feel the same. I think Jidge—we used to call him that—knew more women around the league than the rest of us put together.

Then he started to hit those home runs. Bang, when he hit one, you could hear it all over the park. That's really the first thing I can remember about him—the sound when he'd get

a hold of one. It was just different, that's all.

The thing about Ruth is they never pitched to him. He used to hit home runs on bad balls. When I was over at Cleveland, I remember hearing Speaker tell the pitchers it was all right to walk him with the bases loaded unless it forced in the winning run—better one run than four.

You know the Babe didn't have any education. I remember hearing one of the fellows saying, "Look at that big ignorant ape, making all that money!" I set him straight. We were all making more money because of Ruth. He should have been paid even more money than he was.

What about Harry Frazee. Can you remember him?

[Laughter] Oh, that SOB. He was a tough one! I felt I'd had a great year in 1916—batted over three hundred and hit two home runs in the Series. I was making six thousand dollars and I went in for a raise. We argued for hours (I can still remember that little guy jumping up and down), and finally he said, "I'll tell you what we'll do. We're training in Hot Springs this year. You just got married. Bring your bride down there on the club." I told my wife to take forty baths a day and ride horses the rest of the time. We really stuck Harry on that one!

Can you remember those home runs against Brooklyn in the 1916 Series?

I can remember the one off Jack Coombs. I hadn't been hitting and I was really mad. I actually closed my eyes and swung. Can you believe that—hitting a home run with your eyes closed?

Casey Stengel was managing Boston [National League] back in the forties. I went over to visit with Duffy Lewis, their traveling secretary. I hadn't seen Casey in years. He took one look at me and said, "There's that third baseman that made me show my ass to the crowd chasing those home runs."

How about that famous one-nothing game that Joe Wood won over Walter Johnson in 1912?

Poor Walter. That double that Duffy hit to knock in the run was a real bleeder. They were playing over to the left for Lewis, and he hit a pop fly down the right field line.

But you can't take anything away from Wood that year. My, but he was tremendous, won thirty-four games for us. He threw his arm out though. He was never the same again.

Do you remember Eddie Cicotte when he was with Boston?

A real tragic case. When Eddie was with us, he was always having hard luck. He'd lose two-one, three-two, four-two—all those close games. He wasn't like Carl Mays, always complaining, saying we didn't play hard enough for him. Can you imagine a pitcher saying that? Not Eddie. He was the clubhouse joker, always laughing.

When he left Boston, he developed a hop on his fastball. He'd never tell anybody what it was, but you couldn't hit it.

I always felt sorry for Eddie. He made a bad mistake when he threw those World Series games in 1919 [in the "Black Sox" scandal], and he knew it.

And Carl Mays?

I don't want to say much about Carl. He was a real loner; I don't think he had a friend on the team.

You know I was playing third for Cleveland when he hit Chappie [Ray Chapman]. I was probably the only one in the park who didn't see it. It was a hot day and I'd stuck my head in a bucket of ice water we had on the bench. I heard the thud, and when I looked up there was Chappie on the ground. Ray died the next morning. I never held that against Mays, but I can't say I liked him.

When you were with the Red Sox, you played a lot against Joe Jackson. What kind of a hitter was he?

As good as they come. Nobody hit the ball any harder than Joe. He hit a ground ball in Fenway Park that hit me in the shins. I thought he had broken my leg. After that, I developed a soft kind of felt that I wore under my stockings. It helped a lot.

The pennant race of 1915 was a great one with you and Detroit. What can you remember about it?

Well, I guess it was those games we won from them in September. The Tigers-Red Sox games were always bloody—we all played hard.

I remember one close game when they beat us on a home run by Sam Crawford. I think the pitcher was Dutch Leonard. It looked like Dutch threw him a high fastball. I asked Dutch why he threw a pitch like that to Crawford. He said, "I thought he was going to bunt." Some bunt!

You've given a great interview.

You can't leave til we have a drink.

Have any Cascade whiskey?

[Laughter] I wish I did!

Any plans for the winter? [Here Gardner sprang into his old batting stance.]

I've got to stay in shape: spring training will be coming soon.

Babe Ruth

George Herman Ruth first arrived at Boston in July of 1914. Jack Dunn, owner of the Baltimore International League team had not wanted to lose his 19-year-old star so quickly, but the competition from the Federal League in Baltimore was fierce, almost putting Dunn out of business. He sold Ernie Shore, Ben Egan, and Babe Ruth to Joe Lannin at Boston for $8,500. Egan never made it, but the Babe and Shore turned it into one of the best deals Boston ever made.

Babe got his first start at Cleveland on July 11, when Boston beat the Indians 4-3. He went out for pinch hitter Duffy Lewis in the seventh. It would not be the only time during his pitching life that he was hit for, but each time it happened, the hitter would tell people for the rest of his life, "Hey, I once pinch hit for Babe Ruth."

It wasn't known at the time but this first big league game of the Babe's was to teach him a lesson that would have a dramatic effect on baseball. Cleveland's leading batter was Joe Jackson, the mighty "Shoeless Joe," whose career would end so tragically with the "Black Sox" scandal. Joe collected two hits off Ruth and his batting effort impressed young George immensely. "He had the most natural, smoothest swing," said an admiring Babe. "I began to study and imitate him."

Joe Lannin was also owner of the Providence Clam Diggers in the International League. In order to give Ruth plenty of work and to help the Rhode Islanders win their pennant, Ruth was sent back to the minors. Here he came under the tutelage of the former great Tigers pitcher, "Wild Bill" Donovan and had an opportunity to work on his hitting as well. He learned to place his feet in such a way that he could grip the bat at the end, with his little finger overlapping the handle, and still maintain the full natural swing of Jackson.

By the beginning of the 1915 season, Ruth was ready and so were Bill Carrigan's Red Sox. They won the pennant and World Series. and Ruth accomplished a pitching feat he would talk of for the rest of his life. "I was pitching against the Tigers in a red-hot pennant race," bragged the Babe. "They had the bases loaded with Bob Veach, Sam Crawford, and Ty Cobb coming up. I struck the three of them out. Boy, did Cobb yell. He told the umpire I was doctoring the ball. Ty could really blow up a storm."

Ruth finished the year with an 18-8 record, allowing a mere 6.86

hits per nine innings. He also hit four home runs (an amazing amount for a pitcher when one realizes that outfielder Braggo Roth led the league with seven) and batted .315.

By 1916 he had been acknowledged as the leading southpaw in the league. With 23 wins he was the ramrod on a staff that pushed a modest hitting team to the title. The Red Sox won 91 games and 9 of them were shutouts hurled by Ruth.

"Everyone talks about my hitting; how about my pitching?" asked the Babe. "Do they remember those wins over Walter Johnson?" They should. In the race of 1916, Ruth beat Walter Johnson five straight times, one a 13-inning 1-0 marathon.

For reasons that only Bill Carrigan knew, the Babe had not pitched in the World Series against the Phillies in 1915. He would get his shot against Brooklyn in 1916. In the second game, the Babe pitched 13⅔ scoreless innings, a scoreless Series streak that he extended to 29⅔ innings in the Series of 1918. It was a record not to be broken until Whitey Ford did it against Pittsburgh and Cincinnati in 1960 and 1961.

Boston finished second in 1917 but to no fault of Ruth. He started 38 games, finished a league-leading 35, and piled up 24 victories. His home run tally was a surprisingly low two, but he made 40 hits, and batted .325. He had become not only the Red Sox' leading pitcher but their leading hitter as well.

During the war year of 1918, Red Sox manager Jack Barry was one of the many to join the colors. He was replaced by Ed Barrow. This hard-nosed entrepreneur played a huge part in the Babe's changing from the mound to the outfield. As one after another of the Red Sox left for the service, Barrow found himself desperately pressed for players. When Duffy Lewis left for the navy, he knew he was in trouble. He said to Ruth, "Babe, how would you like to play left field?" The Babe answered in the affirmative. It worked only too well. Babe liked it so much that he wanted to stop pitching altogether, which wasn't exactly what Barrow had in mind. For most of the season the two of them were at swords' points. Barrow wanted two players for the price of one; Ruth wanted to hit.

Meanwhile, Boston and Cleveland

The Red Sox' greatest pitcher.

141

were in a red-hot pennant race and the government had issued its work or fight order. Then word came from Washington—the season would have to end by September 1, but the World Series could be played. Throughout the final month, Barrow pitched Ruth one day and put him in the outfield the next. During the last five weeks of the season, the pitcher-slugger won seven games and led the team in hitting. The Red Sox won the pennant with Ruth winning thirteen games and batting .300. He also won his first home run title, sharing the lead with Tilly Walker of the Athletics. They both hit 11.

He followed the same arduous working pattern in the World Series, pitching and winning two games and playing the outfield for two others. The Red Sox beat the Cubs in six games in a Series remembered mainly for an aborted attempt by the players to strike.

The return of the front line players with the end of the war brought no change in Barrow's plans. In 1919, he used Ruth in the outfield and pitched him whenever he could talk him into it, which was 17 times. The Babe mustered a highly creditable 9-5 record and finished 12 of 15 starts.

It was with his bat that he rewrote the record book and revolutionized the game. Until 1919, the American League home run high had been 16, by Socks Seybold of the Athletics. That mark fell on August 14. The major league record in the century was held by Gavvy Cravath of the Phillies at 24. On Labor Day the Red Sox announced that Ruth would pitch the first game and, in an effort to catch Cravath, play the outfield in the second one. He produced one of the heroic efforts that typified him, winning the first game 2-1 and hitting number 24 in the second game.

Next on the list was Buck Freeman's 25 from the previous century. Ruth tied and broke that mark within the week. It was then discovered that a Ned Williamson had hit 27 with the Chicago White Stockings back in 1884. "What the hell," laughed the Babe, "did they pitch underhand then?" He wasn't far off. That was the year that submarining Charley ("Ole Hoss") Radbourne had won 60 games with Providence.

Owner Harry Frazee decided to have a Babe Ruth Day on September 20. Fittingly, it turned out to be the day the Babe tied old Ned. Number 28 came against the Yankees ("the longest drive ever seen at the Polo Grounds," the newspapers reported), and 29 was belted the last weekend at Washington. The Babe had now hit one in every park during the season—something that had never happened before. His 29 homers were only 1 less than the combined total of the next three top sluggers in the league (George Sisler, Tilly Walker, and Frank Baker) and 25 more than the output of the rest of the Red Sox. He hit four grand slammers, a record that would last for fifty years. With all the home run publicity, it was hardly noticed that his slugging percentage of .657 was also the highest in league history.

It was a truly awesome year, but it was to be his swan song for the crimson hose. He had become the most popular player the Red Sox had ever had to date. If the fans had any idea what a horrendous surprise Mr. Frazee had in store for them, they would have burned down his theaters.

Jimmie Foxx

"Jimmie Foxx could hit a home run over that wall with half a swing."
—Bob Feller

Jimmie Foxx came to the plate one day at Fenway to face the Yankees' Lefty Gomez. "El Goofo" kept shaking off catcher Bill Dickey's signs. Finally, Bill walked out to Gomez. "Just how the hell do you want to

pitch to Foxx?" the exasperated receiver demanded.

"To tell you the truth, I'd rather not pitch to him at all," replied Lefty.

All American League pitchers feared Foxx, Boston's only home run champion between Babe Ruth and Ted Williams. For the six years in which he was the regular first baseman at Fenway, he averaged better than 35 home runs per year. When he hit 50 in 1938, he set the Red Sox' record for most homers in a season and became the only right-handed hitter in the American League to hit 50 or more in two seasons. (He had hit 58 with Philadelphia in 1932.) His 175 RBIs in 1938 placed him first among Red Sox and fourth among major leaguers in single-season RBIs.

With Double X leading the charge, the 1938 Sox leaped from fifth to second place and actually into contention, a heady experience for a club that had been no better than fourth twice in 20 years. They did it

Jimmie Foxx was the brightest Red Sox star in the period between Ruth's departure and WIllliams' arrival.

on awesome hitting. If it were not for Hank Greenberg's 58 home runs and 144 runs scored, Boston players would have all but swept the league lead in every offensive department. Joe Vosmik, the Bohemian from the Cleveland sandlots, led the league in hits with 201, 3 more than the runner-up, Doc Cramer. Cronin led in his specialty, doubles, with 51;

Muscle building—and displaying.

the temperamental Ben Chapman was third with 40. Foxx led in batting average (.349), slugging average (.704), and total bases (398) as well as RBIs. He finished second in home runs and runs scored (139) and third in hits (197). His accomplishments earned him the Most Valuable Player award for 1938. It was his third MVP, and he became the first to gain the honor that often.

It was, of course, the pitching that was lacking. Black Jack Wilson

(ERA 4.30), Fritz Ostermueller (ERA 4.58), Jim Bagby (ERA 4.21), and Footsie Marcum (ERA 4.09), were simply not capable of overtaking the Yankees, who pulled away in August. Only Robert Moses Grove (14-4) was consistent, starting 21 games, finishing 12, and posting a league-leading ERA of 3.08. But Lefty was 38 years old and at that age only Boston's showcase Sunday pitcher.

The late Al Hirshberg gave the accepted opinion of Jimmie: "His personality was one of the gentlest in the game. Foxx hated no one and no one hated him. From the day he first went into the major leagues, he was pleasant to everyone, never impatient with fans or admirers, always accessible to anybody who appreciated him." His greatest fault was that he was too accessible. He was an easy mark for a handout and an overly generous host. He was also too heavy a drinker. He could afford his costly habits as long as the money rolled in, which it did after he left Philadelphia and Connie Mack and began working for Yawkey. But with retirement came financial trouble and grief.

Jimmie's post-baseball days were as dreary as his baseball days had been glorious. He failed with a golf investment in Florida, then as a baseball announcer in Boston (voice too twangy), and in a restaurant venture in Illinois. At one time the former star was reduced to driving a gasoline truck, but a tricky heart condition terminated even this source of income. At age 60, in Florida, a dismal retirement came to a tragic end. The man who had been the Red Sox' chief sustainer in the dreary generation between the departure of Ruth and the arrival of Williams choked to death on a chicken bone.

Ted Williams

"Why, man, he doth bestride the narrow world/Like a Colossus;"
—William Shakespeare in *Julius Caesar*

The overwhelmingly dominant figure of Red Sox baseball is as outspoken and opinionated today as he was during his playing days. And because his was the greatest career not only of any member of the Red Sox but of any baseball player of the era, people still listen in awe. As a senior citizen of the ball field, he would walk into the batting cage in practice, and all eyes, not only in the stands but on the field, would follow him. Today, he talks baseball with as much enthusiasm and authority as ever. He still says with conviction, "Nothing can ever take the place of baseball in my life."

Now 56 years old, Williams works for Sears, Roebuck and Co. and spends much time at his home in Islamorada in the Florida Keys.

Three of the first four Red Sox teams you played on finished second but not close to the Yankees. Where was the Yankee superiority?

Experience, defense, pitching, and probably finesse, but certainly not hitting—we could hit every bit as well as they could if not better. One thing people forget about Joe Cronin is what a strong hitter he was. Did he know hitting and the pitchers in the league! We'd spend hours just talking hitting. If you put Joe at short and Bobby Doerr at second—well, you just couldn't have better hitting up the middle. You just can't say enough about Bobby Doerr.

When you first came up, Jimmie Foxx was the big hitter on the team.

What can you remember about Jimmie?

I stood in awe of him, I really did. I was just a tall, skinny kid, and Foxx had all those muscles. My God, he was strong. When he hit one, well it sounded like an explosion. He was a strong Maryland farm kid. Everybody liked him. He was always grabbing for the check. Poor Jimmie, he never thought the money would stop coming in. He did get drinking quite a bit, but he was one hell of a guy.

How about Grove?

By the time I came up, Lefty had lost his fastball, but he could get them out with skill. You know, it's all a game, a game between the pitcher and the hitter each time. Lefty knew all the ways to play it. I think he won fifteen games that year and he was almost forty years old. He could grumble though. Hell, every time anyone made an error, he'd groan and groan—a real competitor; no one hated to lose more than Lefty. He'd talk to himself out there on the mound.

The thing I remember the most about Grove was his smoothness—very, very graceful. It was a thrill to watch him work, a real pro. I wish I'd seen him in his prime. Do you know who was the fastest left hander I ever saw? Herb Score! He was really fast and getting faster when [the Yankees' Gil] McDougald hit that liner at him. [The line drive struck Score in the face and ruined his career.] He would have been one hell of a pitcher.

Jim Tabor—how about him?

He was another good hitter, but his arm was too strong. He'd pick up a ground ball and throw it fourteen rows back in the stands. His arm was very erratic.

Below: Williams powers one against Chicago at Fenway. *Bottom:* the meat of the order, left to right: Williams, Birdie Tebbetts, Vern Stephens, Dom DiMaggio, Bobby Doerr.

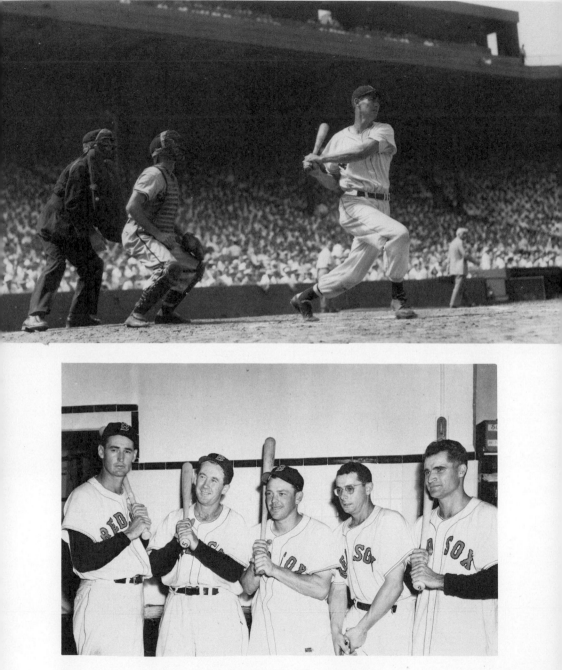

It's been rumored that Jim would take a drink.

Yeah, well I guess that's so. You know, I guess a lot of those guys liked to drink. I never did in those days. Cronin knew [laughter]—he could probably smell it in those little infield meetings they'd have. Not me, I was out in the outfield, but Joe knew who the drinkers were.

What about Rudy York? He had that one great year [1946] with you.

York, he knew all about that little game you play with the pitcher. He was as good at it as anyone. Not only did York have power, but he was a smart hitter—he'd wait for his pitch. York was one of the smartest hitters I ever saw.

Who were some of the good hitters on the Red Sox while you were there?

[Johnny] Pesky and Dominic [DiMaggio] were a couple. They could get good wood on the ball, meet it out front. Dominic made the pitcher pitch; he got a lot of walks. Dominic wanted that pitch where he felt *he* could hit it. [Interestingly, the good hitters Ted remembered were not all sluggers but batters who made good contact with the ball.]

I remember an article that said you hurt the team by walking so much.

The number-one rule on hitting is get a good ball to hit. I'd always give the pitcher that low strike at first. You're better off with one strike than swinging at a pitch when your percentages of getting a hit are small. Don't give that pitcher any more advantages than you have to. I wouldn't swing at a pitch—unless I had two strikes—that I felt I couldn't hit well. Hell, that's the way to hit! I was

bound to get a lot of walks that way, but it was better than grounding out.

Care to comment about some other Red Sox hitters?

Joe Vosmik for one. He used to like his beer, got heavy-legged at the end, but he'd been a real good hitter. And Billy Goodman—he could go with a pitch. Not a great slugger, but he could get wood on it. Want to know who else? Vern Stephens. Hell, he knocked in a hundred fifty-nine runs one year. I had Foxx batting behind me and ahead of me for a while, and Cronin—they were both great hitters, but maybe a little over the hill when I came up. But Vern, he was right on the top of his game when he came over from St. Louis. They pitched to me more often when Stephens was batting behind me than at any other time. Jackie Jensen was good later on, but he didn't get the respect they gave Stephens. I wish he had batted behind me my whole career.

What was your first reaction to the Williams shift?

It all started in the second game of a doubleheader against Cleveland in forty-six. I'd had a great first game, and when I came to bat in the second game, Boudreau had this crazy infield lineup; it seemed everyone was over on the right side. I said, "What the hell is this? He's trying to make a joke out of the game." But I found out it was no joke. I was thrown out on a couple of plays that game that should have been base hits. It hurt me, no doubt about it.

With that shift everybody pulled over to the right side. How is it you still led the league?

They put the shift on in forty-six. In forty-seven I led the league, and

147

in forty-eight. I was barely nosed out in forty-nine and came back to lead again in fifty-seven and fifty-eight. I did pretty good against that damn shift. And I went to left field one hell of a lot more than people remember. I had trouble at first, but I learned how.

When it really hurt was late in the game—the seventh, eighth, or ninth inning. If I came up then, and we were behind, I had to go for the long ball; I had to get it in the air. It was very hard to get a line drive or a ground ball through.

In the last game of the forty-six Series you hit two balls on the button that Walker and Moore caught. Do you remember them?

Hell, I didn't hit them that good. No, I just wasn't hitting, I don't know why. I popped up and I grounded out and I popped up again. I was in a rut and I couldn't unravel.

Did your elbow bother you, the one that had been hurt in the practice game before the forty-six Series?

No, I can't say in my heart that it really bothered me that much. Oh, it was tender the first few days, but the best ball I hit in the Series was against the screen in right—it was foul by a foot—and I hit that in the first game. The one thing I can say about the Series was the wind—it was really bad the four games in Boston. They say, "Well, Slaughter hit one," and yes, he did. But Slaughter hit a high fastball off Tex Hughson that was one of the hardest balls I've ever seen hit. It just kept bucking the wind and finally made the bullpen. Joe Garagiola got a lot of hits, but many of them were banjos. The left-handed hitters didn't really do that well in the Series.

I've always felt it was one of my biggest disappointments that I didn't get in another. Cobb had three World Series and only hit in one.

Of course, Brecheen was really on in that Series, which was another problem for you.

Let me tell you something. Brecheen was great in that Series, had that ball doing just what he wanted. But the next year, in the All-Star Game in Chicago, I hit two blue darters off him—one was a double. But he was *the* pitcher in that Series. Goddamn it, I hate to admit it, but he was beautiful to watch.

What was your biggest disappointment in your career?

Those last two games at Yankee Stadium in forty-nine. Christ, I wanted to beat the Yankees! When that was over, I just wanted to go and hide somewhere. We'd beaten them at Fenway the weekend before; I'd hit two home runs then. Poor McCarthy, he'd taken us from so far behind, and we couldn't win one of them. That really tore me up inside.

148

Above: off to Korea. The plane Williams piloted was hit by anti-aircraft fire, but he returned from mission safely. *Opposite:* Sox' elder statesman counsels rookie Tony Conigliaro.

I'll tell you another blow to me—that elbow injury at the All-Star Game in [July] fifty. I honestly felt I was going to have my best year—had something like eighty RBIs by then—and with plenty of hot-weather baseball left, there's no telling what would have happened. Then I caught this fly against the wall off Ralph Kiner—that was it. It took me until I came back from Korea [in 1953] to really get over that one.

In forty-nine you went down to the wire with George Kell and lost the batting title on the last day. You both hit three forty-three, but Kell won it on a fourth digit. What was your reaction to that?

Kell played the whole game that last day and he had to face Bob Lemon. Now, Lemon was real tough; his ball was acting all over the joint. I think Kell got two or three hits to win it—more power to him. One more hit for me that last day could have also won a pennant, which is a little more important than the batting title.

How did you feel about fifty-four, when you didn't win the batting title because you didn't have four hundred official at-bats? [Williams had 386.]

They said I wasn't a regular. Now how can you not be a regular if you lead the league in walks [129]? I had about thirty home runs. You know, they changed the rule after that. I would have won it under the new rule. What the hell, I won it plenty of times. I got a big kick out of leading the league in fifty-eight; I was forty years old, not bad for an old guy. That's the year I beat out Pete Runnels. He won it later on [1960]; Runnels knew how to get the bat around.

In 1957 you were between thirty-eight and thirty-nine, yet you hit three eighty-eight. I saw a game in Cleveland during that year when Bobby Avila [Indians second baseman] threw you out from the outfield. What do you think you would have hit if you could have run faster?

I'll tell you something. That year I had a total of twelve infield hits, and Mickey Mantle had forty-eight. If I'd had the speed I had ten years before, I would have hit well over four hundred, maybe four-twenty. Yeah, well that was a great year! I was in pretty good shape physically. I did have that damn respiratory problem I used to get toward the end of the season, but all in all, my health was good.

What did you think of McCarthy as a manager?

The best I ever played for. I had more respect for his managerial ability than that of any other manager. It was his presence on the field —that's the way to say it—presence on the field. I can't say I liked him any better or as well as Cronin. I liked Cronin. I liked to play for Cronin, but I thought McCarthy instilled a businesslike attitude in twenty-five guys better than any other manager I ever played for. Another guy like that is Dick Williams.

You think Dick Williams is a good manager?

Absolutely. A businesslike manager; he can instill respect in the players.

How did you rate some of the other managers you played for?

Oh, I'd say they were all right. Lou Boudreau [1952-54] was quite good. I think Steve O'Neill [1950-51] was probably over the hill as a manager; he really wasn't in control. I played for several managers and I've managed myself [manager of the year with Washington in 1969], and I think too many players worry too much about the manager and what he does. When I was out there in the field I always figured, what the

hell, if he changed pitchers, he changed them. Let's get them out and get up and get some runs. The greatest manager in the world isn't going to win without the horses.

Why do you feel the averages aren't as high as they used to be? Is it the slider?

No, the slider can be deadly, but it's been around since the forties. Lemon used it; so did Feller—most good pitchers did.

The coast-to-coast travel is tough; it can upset your whole pattern. There seems to be more demand on the players today. One thing I'm positive of is the lack of stars who really know how to swing a bat. Remember, you've got to study that pitcher, try and figure out what he's going to throw. The longer you can stay up there, the better the chance of getting your pitch. They don't seem to play that little game with the pitcher the way they used to.

I gather you now have no connection with baseball.

That's right. I'm working with Sears on sporting equipment. It's the second most important thing that ever happened in my life.

Would you like to get back into baseball?

Yes, but not as a manager. Hell, last time I put on too much weight; I'd go up in the room and start worrying about the team and just start eating. I called up Joe McCarthy and he said, "You're better than I am; I used to do the same only I'd start drinking." I've never been much of a drinker. What I really would like to do is work with young hitters. There are very few people know as much as I do about hitting.

Johnny Pesky

Johnny Pesky's mission in the Red Sox' battle plan was simple: get on base to be blasted home by the big hitters. For the most part he did and he was. In his first three seasons (1942, 1946, and 1947), he led the league in hits and scored more than 100 runs, usually finishing second or third in the league in runs scored. With the exception of 1948, when he hit .281, he never hit less than .300 with Boston. He reached .335 in 1946 and .324 in 1947. With Pesky setting the table so lavishly, first Williams in 1947, then Vern Stephens and Williams in 1949, and finally Walt Dropo in 1950 won the RBI crown. (In 1946, Williams was runner-up; in 1948, Stephens was.)

But despite the successes, Pesky's big years were tinged with disappointment. In 1946-50, he played on the best teams of the Yawkey era, but they lost two pennants by one game each and a heartbreaking World Series.

His managerial stint in Boston (1963-64) was even less happy. As a player he had had to contend with barely missed triumph; as a manager he never even came close. He did not have good relations with his general manager, Mike Higgins, or with his star, Carl Yastrzemski. Worse, he did not have a good team.

Now in his mid-fifties, Pesky has played, coached, managed (in the majors and minors), and broadcasted. He began his career some 40 years ago as a clubhouse boy with Portland in the Pacific Coast League, and he has no desire to leave baseball. His devotion is complete. "I love this game," he says.

John, you led the league in hits

Johnny Pesky was chief table setter for the Boston sluggers of the forties. He led the league in hits three times.

your first three years with Boston. That was quite a feat with all that power coming up after you. Do you think that batting before sluggers like Williams, Doerr, York, and so on made the pitchers try a little harder to keep you off the bases?

Definitely. Red Rolfe said, "If you can keep Pesky and Dominic off the bases, you can beat those guys."

A hitter like me, or a Nellie Fox —you know, the singles hitter— really earns his base hits. They [the pitchers] don't want me on with the iron coming up. I rarely would get a chance to hit the "cripple," the two-and-nothing or three-and-one pitch. I only had a shot at a three-and-nothing pitch once in my entire career. I can even remember it. It was in 1950 against Washington with Gene Bearden pitching. I stepped out of the batter's box to check the sign, but there it was—hit away. I thought [Steve] O'Neill, who was a good manager, had gone nuts.

What did you do?
I lined out to Mickey Vernon.

The forty-two Red Sox team was never in serious contention, while forty-six was a cakewalk pennant for the team. If you look at both years for you, Ted, Dominic, and Bobby Doerr, they seem to average out. Where was the big difference?

Oh, in the pitching. Hughson was good in both years, but the big difference was Boo Ferriss. Hell, he won a lot of games [25] for us in forty-six. Then there was Dobson, very steady, and Mickey Harris. Don't forget Bob Klinger, great in relief. All in all, it was the best pitching staff we had when I was with the Red Sox. There was also Rudy York. He hit some very timely home runs, but it was mainly the pitching.

When in forty-six did it dawn on you that you could run away with it?

Well, we had those two winning streaks at the beginning [seventeen and twelve straight]. It seems we were always in first place. Then in July, when we had a ten-game lead, we all knew we were in. It was an amazing year. There just didn't seem to ever be any real pressure.

You won the forty-six pennant by twelve games. Everybody was talking about a new Fenway dynasty. Then the bottom fell out in forty-seven. What happened?

Well, once again, it was mainly the pitching. Ferriss, Hughson, and Harris all had arm trouble. Remember, Ferriss had won something like twenty-five games in forty-six and Tex had twenty. I don't think the two of them won twenty-five together in forty-seven [they didn't], and Harris completely collapsed. The only one who stayed on the beam in forty-seven was Joe Dobson. He was a very underrated pitcher, very steady.

And then there was Jake Jones, the first baseman. York went to Chicago and we got Jones. He won the first couple of games for us with home runs. Then he fell apart. They found out he couldn't hit a breaking ball. I could never figure out how a great big guy like that could look so great, then collapse. If I'd had his power, I could have hit forty home runs a year.

Fred Snodgrass died a few months ago at age eighty-six. He always greatly resented the fact that the only thing people remembered about him was the famous thirty thousand dollar muff of 1912. Do you feel the same thing will apply to your famous "holding the ball" in the forty-six World Series?

Pesky slides home safely against the
White Sox, avoiding tag by catcher
Ralph Weigel. Pesky scored more than
a hundred runs six years in a row.

153

Oh, I suppose so, but it really doesn't bother me that much. You know, Dominic had gone out and Lee Culberson was in center. I saw the films again the other day—he really lobbed the ball to me. Remember, I had gone out to short left to get it. I would have needed a rifle to nail Slaughter. The film shows I really didn't hold it at all. But, as I said, it really doesn't bother me.

You lost the forty-eight pennant in the playoff against Cleveland. But every loss during the season turned out to be just as costly. Does any one game stick in your mind that you feel you should have won?

Yes, actually two of them, the doubleheader we lost to the A's on Patriot's Day. I didn't get a hit in either game.

We opened up the second inning of the first game with a bang, three straight home runs—Stan Spence, Vern Stephens, and Bobby Doerr. We're ahead three to nothing and still nobody out. Phil Marchildon was pitching for Mack. We thought Connie would pull him, but he didn't. From then on, we were helpless. The A's kept chipping away at Joe Dobson and finally tied it. We lost it in the eleventh inning, five to four, and the run we got in the last of the eleventh was a gift. I've never seen a pitcher come back off the ropes the way Marchildon did.

The second game wasn't any better. Lou Brissie—you know, the war hero (he'd had his leg all shot up in Italy)—pitched a great game, but we still should have won. I remember that Vern Stephens made a costly error. Actually, Brissie won the game himself with a single with the bases loaded. That was the game Ted lined one of those bullets off Brissie's bad leg. We all knew what Lou

had been through; everyone was sure he was finished for good. But the guy hung in there and beat us four to one.

There will always be a controversy over Joe McCarthy's picking Denny Galehouse for the playoff with Cleveland in forty-eight. Al Hirshberg has said that both Mel Parnell and Ellis Kinder would have loved to have pitched it. What did you feel at the time?

Mel has said he would have loved to have pitched it? That's news to me! I never heard Mel say that. And Kinder certainly didn't have it. Remember, he came in after Galehouse and was no puzzle.

I think Cleveland would have beaten anybody that day. Hell, Lou Boudreau hit two home runs and got two other hits; he was always doing something. We only made five hits off Bearden—that was our real problem. We were just never in that ball game.

It's a funny thing, we kept thinking we'd get to Bearden but we couldn't do it. When it was all over, Ted said, "That guy will never win twenty again in the majors; he'll be lucky to have another winning season." [Ted was right. His best record after 1948 was eight and eight.]

The 1949 season must have been like a rerun of a Boris Karloff movie. Once again you lost it on the last day. Can you remember any one game that you should have won?

That series—the end of June when Joe DiMaggio came back to the lineup. We were hot, had a couple of recent winning streaks, and had our top pitchers ready for them.

We'd had a lousy start that year [Boston was twelve games out by June], but now we were really moving.

154

Opposite top: an accomplished shortstop.
Opposite bottom: nabbing Cards' Schoendienst at second in 1946 Series.

The Yankees beat [Mickey] Mc-Dermott the first game in a close one with DiMaggio hitting his first home run of the year. It was the second one we should have won, but it turned into a nightmare.

We opened up with a barrage of hits and four runs in the first and should have had more. Ellie Kinder came up with the bases loaded and lined one back at the pitcher. I can't remember who he was—we'd already knocked out Tommy Byrne. [It was Clarence ("Cuddles") Marshall.] In any case, the pitcher knocked it down. Rizzuto picked it up, stepped on second, and threw to first for a freak double play.

Then we came right back with two more runs in the second. Ted bunted toward third and easily beat it out. Vern Stephens followed with one into the screen. By the middle of the game we had them down seven to one with Kinder pitching. Ellie may have liked his bourbon, but he sure could pitch. We felt we had this one all locked up.

What we forgot about was Joe Di-Maggio. He belted two home runs. One of them went over the wall, the screen, and everything; it might have gone all the way to the Hotel Kenmore for all I know.

Ted Hughson had come in and had nothing. I think Joe hit his last homer off Earl Johnson. In the meantime Stengel had brought in Joe Page and we couldn't do anything. We lost it nine to seven.

Mel Parnell lost another tough one the next day. I think DiMaggio hit another, but it was that second game of the series we should have won. Like I said, it was a nightmare.

You played shortstop for three years next to Bobby Doerr. You might recall the perennial question, **"Who was the better second baseman, Doerr or Gordon?" It was a big issue in New England and New York. What is your opinion?**

I'd have to go with Bobby. Gordon was an outstanding second baseman, but Doerr was the best in the league while I was playing.

His disposition was ideal for a ball player. He never bitched, just did his job and did it great. You could always count on Bobby to come through in a pinch. Really, he was one of the best players I ever saw, at bat and in the field.

What three pitchers gave you the most trouble?

Well, there was Early Wynn, but I got so I hit him pretty good. The toughest was probably old Ted Lyons. He threw that slow stuff. I never figured him out. It's a good thing for me that he wasn't ten years younger. I remember distinctly, I was nothing for eighteen against him.

Then there was Allie Reynolds and Vic Raschi. Those Yankee pitchers always gave me a hard time. Dizzy Trout at Detroit, he was also tough.

Who was the greatest hitter you ever played with or against?

It has to be Ted, but Joe DiMaggio was great also. I'd love to see Ted back in baseball. The game needs him. If Ted were to manage again, I'd call him and offer to go back on the field as a coach. He's one of the truly great people.

When Kasko was fired, I'd hoped that the Red Sox would make an offer to Ted, but they didn't. I think that Mr. Yawkey would have liked Ted to have asked for the job and he probably would have gotten it. But I guess it won't happen.

In June of fifty-two you were traded

As a manager of the Red Sox, Pesky
had to contend with Dick Stuart
(capless *below*) and other losers.

to Detroit with Walt Dropo, Fred Hat-
field, Bill Wight, and Don Lenhardt
for Dizzy Trout, George Kell, Hoot
Evers, and John Lipton. You were
thirty-two at the time and had spent
all of your career in the Red Sox organization. How did you feel?

I felt bad—one of the reasons
being we were in first place at the
time. We all felt we had a chance to
win it.

Dropo and Lenhardt were right at
the top of the league in RBIs. Don
had won the game over Chicago the
day before with a grand slam. Afterward they said that almost killed the
deal.

You're supposed to be rejuvenated
by a trade, but it didn't work with
me—even though I had a pretty
good year in fifty-three.

Actually, Kell was supposed to be
the key, but I don't think he lasted
two years with Boston. Walt was the
sad part. He kicked around the majors for close to ten years after the
trade. I know he'd have done much
better if he'd stayed at Boston.

When Vern Stephens came over
to the Red Sox with Jack Kramer
[one of the Red Sox' best trades] in
November of forty-seven, you were
asked to move from short to third.
Did this bother you?

No, not really. Oh, I would have
preferred to have stayed at short.
But as long as I could play and it
helped the team, it was fine with me.

We had Sam Dente, Eddie Pellagrini, and several other guys at third
in forty-seven. There's no question
but that we were a much better
team with Junior [Stephens] at short
and me at third in forty-eight. We
couldn't have gone as far as we did
without the move.

You know O'Neill switched us in
fifty-one; Vern at third and me back

at short. Do you remember that record he set at third—I think it was
for assists. [On May 23, 1951,
Stephens had 10 assists in a game,
most for an American League third
baseman until Ken McMullen of
Washington got 11 on September
26, 1966.] Well, it was in the ninth
inning, we were playing the Browns,
and there was a hard ground ball
hit to me. We all knew he needed
one more for the record, so I quickly
flipped to Vern and he fired to first
and got the guy out. Junior was a
hell of a great guy; he died too soon.

When you became manager, you
replaced Mike Higgins, who became
general manager. The word was that
you and Higgins had problems.
Were the rumors exaggerated?

157

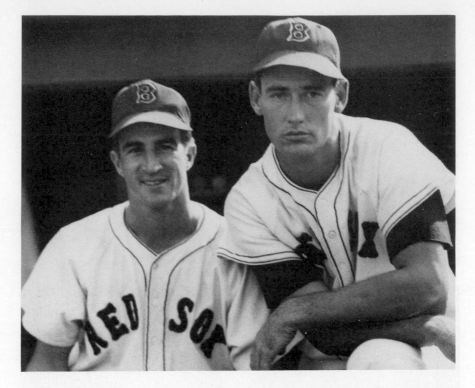

I'm sure they were *not*. If anything, underrated. I was in trouble from the beginning with Pinky. He wanted Yogi Berra as manager, but Mr. Yawkey wanted me. I had hoped that Higgins would forget about it once I was manager, but he never really did.

You know, Mike and I had been teammates, third and shortstop, in forty-six. I had thought we were friends, but I just can't say we were while I managed. I always felt he was cutting me up. Mike is gone now and I don't want to be unfair. But, the fact remains he didn't want me as manager when I got the job and he never really did accept me.

There was a lot of publicity while you managed about trouble between you and Dick Stuart. What about it?

Dick was ten years too soon with Boston. He would have been a great DH. He really could hit—tremendous power, a very strong guy. But out on the field he was a menace. Just didn't have any interest at all. Nobody could hit well enough to make up for what he cost us in the field. He'd just wave at balls.

Don't get me wrong; it was impossible not to like Dick—a tremendous sense of humor, never took anything seriously. He was always telling me I'd be lucky to bat two hundred against the pitching in the sixties. Then, he was always saying, "John, did you ever hit a home run?" But, if you took the bat out of Stuart's hand, he wasn't even a good semipro player.

158

Carl Yastrzemski

Sometimes a player does so well in one year that he becomes identified with it: Dizzy Dean in 1934, Joe DiMaggio in 1941, and Denny McLain in 1968, for example. It happened to Yaz in 1967 to such an extent that many forget about his other years. "Yaz was just phenomenal," says Dick Williams. "He did everything that year—hitting, running, fielding, throwing, hitting with power, everything—and he did it consistently. I played with some other great players with the Dodgers—Robinson, Hodges, Campy, Snider—but I never saw anyone have the year that Carl had in sixty-seven."

Of course, Carl has been the mainstay of the Red Sox in every other of his 14 seasons as well. It began in 1961, when he was the much-touted rookie who was to replace the retiring deity in left field. Since then he has won two batting crowns in addition to the one in 1967 (his Triple Crown year) and missed another by less than a percentage point. Somewhat less prolific now, he still leads the club as its stellar senior citizen.

When he is finished, Carl will probably have more hits and have played more games than any other member of the Red Sox. Except for 1967, he has not equaled Ted, but

Yaz fouls one off.

then deities are somewhat scarcer these days.

Carl, when you joined the Red Sox in sixty-one, Ted Williams had just retired. You were being touted as the next superstar for Boston. Do you feel this presented more pressure for you than the normal rookie?

Absolutely—no question about it. I had come up fast in the minors, had signed for a large bonus, and had received all this publicity. The writers and the fans were watching every move. The pitchers were the toughest. They become very aware of you. A rookie without the big buildup has it much easier.

Several teams had put in a bid for your services. Any special reason why you picked the Red Sox?

It came down to the Phillies and the Red Sox. I went down to Philadelphia and took a great deal of bat-

ting practice at Connie Mack Stadium. It was beautiful, a much better park for a left-handed hitter.

I'm sure I would have hit well in Philly. Father Joe, a family friend, pointed out two key things about the Red Sox. First, he considered them the lousiest team in baseball, and second, they had the greatest owner in baseball. I felt I'd have a good chance of making the team in a hurry at Boston and the money was right, so I signed.

Can you give any other reactions to your rookie year?

Well as I said, there was the pressure. My average was down around two hundred and I had serious doubts if I could make it. Remember, I was only twenty-one years old. I started fooling around with my stance. I had hit more in a crouch like Musial. I straightened up more. The second half of the year I began

160

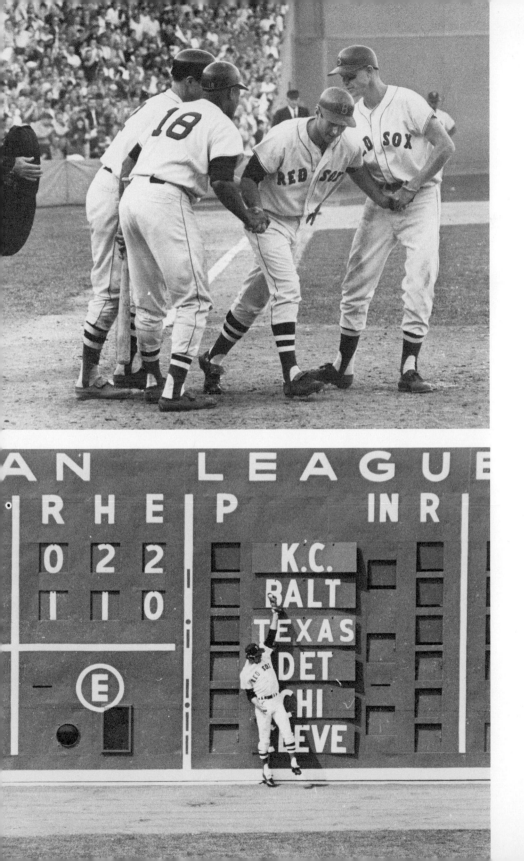

players but not the kind of manager to make big things happen. Remember, he had lousy teams. A very non-controversial manager. He would have been an excellent manager for a team with strong talent.

For many years there has been this thing about the "country club" atmosphere of the Red Sox. How does this affect you and the rest of the team?

It's a lot of baloney. [Yaz didn't say baloney.] The writers have always found it an easy generalization to put down the players. The reason we didn't do much the first six years I was on the team was we had lousy players—just plain lack of talent. We're no different than any other team. We have a great owner but that certainly does not hurt the team's ability. After all, we're pros. This is how we make our living and the better we play the better the living.

Now that you have well over two thousand hits, close to three hundred home runs, and a good chance to have more base hits than any other Red Sox, what is your attitude toward reaching these milestones?

Well, of course I want them, especially the three thousand hits.

to make good contact and my confidence returned. Actually, my rookie year called for adjustment both off the field and on.

Outside of Joe Cronin, Pinky Higgins spent more time as manager of the Red Sox than any other manager. What was Pinky like?

A very patient man. Without patience he would not have stuck with me as long as he did that first year. He kept trying to restore my confidence. He was great with young

How many years do you think it will take you after this year?

Four or five, if I stay healthy.

You were just about as close a friend as Reggie Smith had on the Red Sox. He seems now to be headed for superstar status. While he had some great years with Boston, he was never a superstar. Why?

Reggie is very sensitive. The negative attitude of the sportswriters and the fans booing really hurt him—

especially when the booing came when he was hurt and tried to play. When he'd try to run and couldn't get up steam, it'd look as if he wasn't trying and he was.

He could easily be the MVP over in that league. He's a great low ball hitter—you can't throw one by him. With all the AstroTurf they have, he's going to hit a lot of ground balls that'll go through for base hits.

A lot has been written about Ted Williams teaching you how to hit. Care to comment?

No one can *teach* you how to hit. Ted can help a great deal. He knows more about hitting than anyone else. He's a great theorist and he loves to talk hitting. There's no question but that he helped me a great deal. Especially when I was slumping. He can always pick out what's wrong. Then it's up to you to see if you can correct it.

You have played under five managers, excluding Johnson. If you owned a team, who would you want for a manager?

Well, the first six years the teams were so bad you really can't judge if the managers were any good or not. You really just can't make a fair appraisal.

I loved Kasko. He would be a great manager with a good team. No controversy. As for a making-things-happen type of manager, I'd have to pick Dick Williams. He was a doer.

You won the pennant in sixty-seven with that last series against Minnesota. The year before you had lost more games than any other team in the American League. When did you feel you had a serious shot at the pennant?

It was the ten-game winning streak in July. We had lost six games—three in California and three in De-

Opposite: pennant pressure, 1967.
Above: Series joy—with Lonborg after Jim beat Cards 5-0 and Yaz drove in four.

LEAGUE · NATIONAL LEAGUE

P IN R P IN R P IN R P IN R

29 K.C.
30 N.Y.
BALT
CLEVE
38 CAL 2 1
21 DET 2 2

27 WASH
20 CHI
UMPIRES
3 13 7

23 HOUS 1 0
13 PITT 3
23 CHI 1 0
17 CIN 3
1 ST.L.
19 ATLA

N.Y.
L.A.
PHIL
S.F.

troit. It looked as if we would fall apart. Then came those ten games around the All-Star break and all those people greeting us at the air-port. We knew then we could stay in it right down to the end.

On the other hand, you lost the divisional title the last series of the year against Detroit in seventy-two. Where was the turning point that year?

It had to be that first game of the series against Detroit, when Lolich weathered the first inning. You have to get Lolich early and we really had him on the ropes. If we had won that one, and we should have, we would have been certain to win one of the next two.

What has been your number-one thrill in baseball?

Those entire last three months of sixty-seven. We were up for each

game, and then we had to keep track of what the other teams were doing. It was my first real race and I've never seen anything quite like it. The last two games against Min-nesota were, of course, the climax.

In 1970, you lost out on your fourth batting title on the last day of the season. They had to figure it out to a fourth digit. Alex Johnson won with point three two eight nine against your point three two eight six. What was your reaction?

I had read in the paper where he said he would play the entire last game. He didn't. If I had known he wasn't going to, I might have come out when I was one for two. There would have been no way that he could have caught me if I had. I later found out that his manager [Lefty Phillips] had taken Alex out, but I still wish he hadn't. I would liked to have won it.

What three pitchers in the American League would you rather not have pitching against the Red Sox in a game that could decide the pennant?

A lot more than three. Lolich would be one. If you don't get him early, you don't get him. He's tremendous in the clutch. [Wilbur] Wood is another. You have a great deal of trouble hurting him. He can always get you on the stuff he throws, even if you've been hitting him. And [Nolan] Ryan. As fast as he is, if he's really on, he simply overpowers you.

You had been captain of the team in the mid-sixties and then relinquished it when Dick Williams became manager. Now you're captain again. Any difference?

Yes, definitely. The first time it was on and off the field. I found myself the sounding board for all the complaints—kind of a middleman between the players and the manager. Every time anyone had a bitch about anything, they'd come to me.

I was also a lot younger then. This time it is understood that my job is only between the baselines. I only get involved in what is going on out on the field.

The Yastrzemski clan has recently bought a big potato spread down in Maine. Does this mean potato farming is on the way down on Long Island?

It sure does. Between taxes, labor, and available land, it is not what it used to be.

Do you intend to spend much time working in Maine?

I've always liked the outdoors. I'll be helping a lot with the digging, particularly when we're setting it up. It's a great life!

Opposite: this time the wall wins. *Above left and right:* two toughies—Nolan Ryan of California and Wilbur Wood of Chicago.

Rico Petrocelli

Rico Petrocelli joined the Red Sox organization as quickly as he dispatches hanging curve balls into the left field screen. "Bots Neekola took me and my family to Fenway," he recalls. "We were so impressed by Mr. Yawkey and how well they treated us that I said 'This is it'."

Since then it hasn't always been as smooth. After working his way through the minors, he became the regular Boston shortstop under Billy Herman in 1965, overcoming an uncommonly strong lack of confidence. As an established player he came to chafe at the traveling demands baseball made on him. (He is a family man with four sons, including twins.) The most bizarre controversy in which he was involved stemmed from the allegation of an airline stewardess that he had molested her. "Of all the guys to pick, she goes after Rico," said an incredulous teammate. "She must be some kind of a nut." The incident was ridiculous to many (Rico went to court and was acquitted) but not to Rico. Then in 1974, a year that began brilliantly ended dismally. On July 30, he was hitting .307 with fourteen home runs and 56 RBIs. Then came the famine for him as well as for the rest of the team. He batted less than .200 for the rest of the year and hit only one home run.

The controversies have sometimes obscured the accomplishments, of which there have been many. In 1969, Rico's bonanza year with Boston, he hit .297, had a slugging percentage of .589, and established the American League home run record for a shortstop, 40. Two years later, when the Red Sox sent Mike Andrews to Chicago for Luis Aparicio,

Rico was moved to third, where he promptly played 77 consecutive games without an error, a league record. As of the end of the 1974 season, he was Boston's fifth leading all-time home run hitter (and only one strong season from third) and its second most durable infielder of all time. He has played 10 seasons of 100 or more games, second only to Bobby Doerr.

Nevertheless, because of his dislike of travel, his end-of-season slump, and an elbow injury he incurred on September 15 when Jim Slaton of Milwaukee hit him with a pitch, Rico has spoken seriously of retirement—again. The Red Sox hope they can dissuade him again. Thirty-one years of age is just too soon for a player of his talents to quit.

After you signed with Boston, you played in three minor leagues. How were they; do you think they discourage a young player?

Of the three the toughest was the Eastern League. Those long bus trips are murder. The Carolina League wasn't bad; the towns are close, no long trips. The Coast League was tremendous. We flew jets all the time. We'd fly to Hawaii, which was beautiful. The only bad one was the Eastern—lousy hotels, lighting wasn't very good. It was rough, but remember, you really want to play ball or you wouldn't be there. I can't really say it hurts any young players; they're mainly too concerned about trying to move up.

In your first two years [1965 and 1966] the Red Sox were certainly not a good team. On the other hand, in 1967, 1972, and 1974, you've been on contenders. What is the basic difference between the two types of teams?

Those first teams had some individuals who played well and some veterans who could return to form on occasions. We also had some young players like myself, George Scott, Tony C., and Lonborg; we were getting better each year. The overall pitching just wasn't there. The hitting wasn't bad [the Red Sox were second in the league in 1965, though they lost 100 games], but we couldn't hold leads. The main problem was the attitude—it was a losing one. We couldn't play together as a team. It became a grind to come to the park every day. It's not much fun when you always lose the close ones.

Then came sixty-seven and everything changed; the game became alive again. It was then that I realized that the main thing was to win the pennant. I don't think I really became a big leaguer until then.

It has been said that the left field

Top: Rico fires to first to double up Tigers. *Above:* Petrocelli was the first American League shortstop to hit 40 homers in a season. Here he displays prized fortieth home run ball, September 29, 1969.

167

Career highpoint: bombing Dick Hughes in the sixth game of the 1967 World Series.

wall hurts a lot of the young players coming up because they try to pull everything. Do you agree?

I don't think it hurts the young players coming up in the Red Sox chain; they're given the word not to break their back trying to pull everything. As for the left handers, like [Cecil] Cooper and [Rick] Miller, they can go with the outside pitch and hit the wall.

What it did hurt was some of the veterans who were traded here when I first came up. It was late in their careers and they tried to pull the ball more than they had before. Very few could do it, and I think they really suffered.

On June 10, 1974, against Vida Blue, you hit a rising ball that hit the wall. You ended up with a double. Do you remember it?

Yes, I certainly do.

Do you feel you lose many home runs because of the wall?

Yes, I do. There are several balls that just make the net and someone will say, "Oh, what a cheap shot!" What they forget is most of them are so high up they'd be out of a lot of other ball parks. What you do get is a lot of base hits against the wall that might be caught in other parks, but home runs, no—you lose as many as you get; they even each other out.

What do you consider your biggest day with the Red Sox?

Oh, that sixth game of the World Series in sixty-seven. We were down three-two in games, and I hadn't been hitting. Lonborg had won the fifth game in St. Louis, and we were back in Fenway. Dick Hughes was pitching for them, and we had Gary Waslewski.

The first time up I put us ahead one to nothing with a home run. Then they came back with a couple of runs in the third. Lou Brock stole a base; he was always doing that.

Yaz opened the fourth with a blast into the bleachers. Then with two down, Reggie Smith hit another. I followed Reggie in the order. I was really surprised when they gave me another fastball, and I tore into it. Those two home runs, plus our winning the game, were my biggest thrills, no doubt about it.

What about sixty-nine, when you hit the forty home runs and broke Vern Stephens' record?

What a year—everything went right, every ball I hit. I hit pitches that were good pitchers' pitches, low and away, up and in. It was amazing—I wasn't doing anything different; it all just seemed to come together for that year.

You have the reputation of having quick wrists. Do you think this is really important in hitting?

Yes, definitely; you have to get the hands through, hit the ball out in front. There's a lot more to it—timing and concentrating—but if you make good contact out in front, it's bound to go.

Long a shortstop, you are now considered one of the best fielding third basemen in the league. Which of the two do you prefer, short or third?

It'd be tough for me to go back to short, but I do prefer the position. That is where I started. The reason I went over to third was because Eddie Kasko couldn't get a third baseman and he could get Louie Aparicio. Actually, I would have gone anywhere the Red Sox asked me to. Playing next to Louie was really great, one of my best experiences in baseball.

Would you care to comment on that accusation from the stewardess?

It was absolutely untrue, a big fairy tale. I can't understand why she would do that; I guess she has some kind of a problem. I'm the one who eventually got it to court; I'd been trying for a year or so. The whole thing certainly shattered my trust in human nature.

Your whole career has been loaded with threats to quit or acknowledged requests to be traded. Care to comment on that?

My biggest problem has been the traveling. We have a very close family. I'm just not the type of guy who should travel. It's never been anything about the Red Sox. This is really a first-class organization, especially Mr. Yawkey. I can't remember one guy who's been treated badly by the team. I thought for a while if I was traded it might be better, but I'd still have the travel. It would be tough without baseball, though. It's a great game and I owe everything to it.

Tommy Harper

In 1912, a glorious year for the Red Sox, Tris Speaker pillaged 52 bases. This team record stood until 1973, when Tommy Harper stole 54. Particularly in the second half of the season, Tommy produced at a truly superstar level for Boston. In this period he hit a lusty .324, hit 14 of his 17 home runs, and produced 46 of his 71 RBIs. His efforts were a major factor in the run that Boston made at Baltimore for the pennant. The Red Sox won 8 games in a row in August, only to be stymied by the Orioles' 14-game streak. For his contributions during the stretch, the Boston baseball writers voted Harper the Red Sox' most valuable player for 1973.

Tommy was an established artist in the base stealing trade long before he came to the Red Sox. Upon his arrival he was already one of five players to have stolen more than 30 bases and hit more than 30 home runs the same year. His 73 steals with Seattle in 1969 were the most in the American League since Ty Cobb's 96 in 1915.

Barring injuries, he will undoubtedly end his career with more than 400 stolen bases and perhaps as many as 500. But his main ambition, to play in a World Series, may be more difficult to realize. At 34 he may have few more chances left to reach the Series, and with Boston's wealth of young outfielders he will have to battle to keep his job. [Ed. Note: in December 1974 Harper was traded to California for Bob Heise.]

Tommy, you're almost thirty-four years of age, and Lou Brock is thirty-five. Yet both of you seem to be able to steal bases as well as ever. Surely you can't be as fast as you were ten years ago. How do you continue to be such a good base stealer?

Conditioning is vital. I watch my diet very carefully and run a lot. Of course, the main thing is experience. The longer you're around, the more you know the pitchers—who can hold you on, who you can get a jump on. Base stealing is a real specialty; it takes a great deal more than just speed.

What do you consider the ideal stealing situation?

First, there's the automatic, the three and two pitch. You know I'm always going on that. Then there's the flow of the game. If I'm on first and the game is close, I'll be always looking for that opening. Of course, this can also upset the pitcher. He knows I may be going, and it can rattle him. Remember, every time he throws to first, there's a chance he'll throw it away.

You also have to take into consideration the batter. For instance, take Rico. He very rarely gets a fastball. With those quick hands of his, they can't throw it by him. He's very apt to get a breaking pitch or a change-up. They're easier to steal on than the fastball. The chances are very good I'll be going down with Rico up.

Then there's the out situation. Say I'm on first, two outs, and someone who gets a lot of singles comes up. If I make it, I'm in scoring position. If not, the good hitter starts the next inning.

Can you remember anyone who helped you in base stealing when you were coming up?

No, not really. When I first started, I had the speed. The experience you have to get on your own.

Who do you think is the toughest catcher as far as throwing you out is concerned?

I think the best catcher in the league is Carlton Fisk. I'm glad I don't have to run on him. Actually, [Thurman] Munson does not have that good an arm, but he's extremely fast in getting the ball away. Ellie Rodriguez is another one who can get you. Some catchers are tougher for certain runners. I notice where Lou Brock recently said [Jerry] Grote was tough for him. I never had that much trouble with Grote.

Do you steal on the pitcher or the catcher?

Oh, no doubt about it, you steal on the pitcher. I'll go on any catcher if I can get the jump on the pitcher. As good as Fisk is, two of the reasons he can keep the steals down are [Luis] Tiant and [Bill] Lee. They have that quick throw over to first. They'd be real tough to get the jump on.

Baseball seems to have had a tremendous renaissance in base stealing in the sixties and seventies. Jackie Jensen led the league in fifty-four with twenty-two, Dominic DiMaggio in fifty with only fifteen. Any special reason for this increase?

Yes, I think it was Maury Wills. Maury didn't have much power, but when he got on, the defense had to be on their toes. They particularly didn't want him opening up an inning. I even remember them walking [Sandy] Koufax with two outs so Wills wouldn't be the first one up the next inning. It dawned on the managers that when someone like Wills could get a walk, it was like a double or even a triple.

You have been an outstanding base stealer in both the American and National Leagues. Any difference between the two as far as getting that jump is concerned?

I don't thing so. They're both majors—sometimes you can get the jump and sometimes you can't in both. I remember watching Johnny Bench come up my last year at Cincinnati. He's got a great arm, but I feel I could steal on him if I had the good jump. Same with the good ones in the American League.

Fenway Park is natural grass. Do you think this helps or hinders bunting as compared with AstroTurf?

Well, of course it helps it. The bunt does move faster on the Astro-Turf. But, then again, the infield plays in closer on the natural grass. I believe one probably crosses out the other.

You're one of the best bunters. Anyone help you here?

Yes, Maury Wills. I remember him saying, "Tommy, you're committing too soon with your back foot. You've gotta keep that the same as if you're hitting away until the last minute. The infielders will watch that foot, and the instant you move it, they start coming in on you." Maury was the best bunter I ever saw—I used to study him every chance I had.

What has been your biggest thrill in baseball?

I can honestly say coming to the ball park every day. I'm doing something that I've always wanted to do, and there are millions of others who have wanted to but couldn't. What I'm really looking forward to is playing in a World Series. In sixty-four, when I was with Cincinnati, we came close, and seventy-two really broke me up. I thought we had it for sure.

Dwight ("Dewey") Evans

Dewey Evans has been playing professional baseball for five years, since he was 17. Like most major leaguers, he loves the game and the money he gets for playing it. In 1974, he gave the Red Sox their money's worth by hitting close to .300, playing right field with the ardor of a rookie but the composure of a veteran, and throwing with the power and accuracy of a Carl Furillo.

Dewey loves to hit, but he is also conscientious in polishing his other skills. Early in the 1974 season he found himself platooned often, but as the season progressed he became more and more firmly planted in right field. Barring catastrophe, he should be there for some time.

You have the reputation of being a hustler. Do you feel this type of play pays off very much?

Yes, and it makes me feel good. I'm going to give a hundred and ten percent every minute I'm on the field. It's the only way I want to play. Playing baseball is the greatest thing in the world to me. And I'll tell you something else: it really burns me up when I see some guy not hustling who makes a lot more money than I do.

You have a great arm—has it always been that good or did you develop it throughout your career?

Well, I guess I have a better than average arm. It has always been strong, but it used to be very wild. I used to throw too hard. Now I try and take a little off the ball and still get it away as quickly as possible. Getting it away fast is extremely important. Actually, I've spent a lot of time practicing it.

172

You beat Fritz Peterson one to nothing at Yankee Stadium on the second of July in 1973, with a home run to right field. On the tenth of June in 1974, you hit a three-run homer to right off Vida Blue at Fenway. Have you always been able to hit to right with that much power?

An inveterate hustler, Evans upsets Brewers' John Vukovitch and their double play.

Yes. Actually, I used to hit to right more often than I do now. When I was at Greenville, I would hit to right most of the time—couldn't get around as fast as I do now. Now when I hit to right, it's because I go with the pitch. Blue's pitch was low and away.

In 1972, you had a perfectly dreadful first half at Louisville, hitting about one-ninety. Then, the second half you tore the cover off the ball. Your final average was three hundred. You led the league in RBIs and were voted the league's MVP. What happened?

173

It was a big jump from the Carolina League to the International. The pitching was much better. The main reason was just plain pressing. It seemed the worse I hit, the more I pressed. Darrell Johnson [Louisville manager in 1972] told me to calm down, that my problem was mental. I figured I had nothing to lose, so I said the hell with it and just relaxed.

Our next game was at Rochester —I think Jesse Jefferson was pitching. I went four for four that day and from then on I was on a real tear. At one point, I was forty-two for sixty-eight. You just can't press when you're hitting; you have to stay loose.

You were then called up from Louisville and arrived at Fenway in the middle of a torrid pennant race. What are your recollections about that?

Oh, that doubleheader with Baltimore [on August 20, 1972]. It was the biggest thing I'd ever seen. We won both games. I got four hits, two in each game. After [Marty] Pattin beat [Jim] Palmer in the first one, [Luis] Tiant and [Mike] Cuellar went in the second. Cuellar had put me out twice and had two strikes on me when I timed one of those screwballs for a triple. Then I hit a home run off [Eddie] Watt the next time up. We all really thought we were in then. Of course, I remember those games in Detroit, but why talk about them?

Other than Darrell Johnson, can you remember any managers who helped you when you were in the minors?

Yes, Sam Mele helped me a great deal. I was only eighteen. He was a tremendous help in getting me to adjust to minor league baseball. And Don Lenhardt. Not only did he really know how to play the outfield, but he knew how to teach. I learned a great deal from Lenhardt.

What do you consider your greatest game as a Red Sox?

It was against California right here in Fenway sometime around the end of May last year [May 29, 1973]. We beat California two to one for Tiant. I went three for three and knocked in one of the runs. Before that I'd been in a bad slump and so had the team. I don't even think we were at five hundred. That was the game when Al Gallagher knocked Fisk over in a crucial play at the plate, but Carlton held the ball. Gallagher was out.

Tiant let a couple go at Gallagher. You know Louie. He said, "I back up our players." Louie doesn't throw at them very often, but he did that night. I think Gallagher and Fisk had a fight. [They did.]

The thing I remember most was the catch on [Mike] Epstein in the ninth inning. I think it was the best I've ever made. It was going to be a home run, no doubt about it. Louie was sure happy. He said, "Wow, you make great catch for me!" When someone like Luis says that to you, it makes you feel good all over.

Did you ever hear of Larry Doyle?
No.

He was a second baseman of John McGraw's when the Giants were winning a lot of pennants. He said, "It's great to be young and be a Giant!" With the possibility of a lot of Boston titles in the near future, could you say the same thing about the Red Sox?
Absolutely!

174

123456789

OFF THE WALL

some screwballs, curve balls, and oddballs

On June 23, 1917, Eddie Shore pitched a perfect game for the Red Sox, though he was not the starting pitcher. He came in after Babe Ruth had opened the game against Washington by walking Eddie Foster. Ruth objected so strenuously to the umpire's call on the fourth ball (he belted the arbiter) that he was thrown out. Foster was then thrown out himself (stealing), and Shore was perfect the rest of the way.

In 1927, Boston traded Emory Rigney to Washington for Buddy Myers. By 1928, Rigney was out of the majors, while Myers hit .313 and led the American League in stolen bases. It was one of the best trades in Red Sox history. Not used to such a windfall, the Red Sox traded Buddy back to Washington in 1929.

Earl Webb established the single-season record for doubles with 67 in 1931. The rumor persists in Boston that as he neared the record he stopped at second on some sure triples.

On June 27, 1923, Cleveland beat Boston 27-3, in a game that has been referred to as "the Indian Massacre." In the sixth inning of that game, a Red Sox pitcher, as it were, gave up 13 runs, and shortly after this misadventure he was released. It took him five years to work his way back to the majors, and when he finally returned it was to the National League as an outfielder. Somewhat more successful in his new role, Frank ("Lefty") O'Doul twice led the league in hitting, with averages of .398 and .368.

As for simple mistakes in judging talent, the Red Sox can claim Pie Traynor, whom they rejected in a tryout; Babe Herman, who was on their roster but never got into a game; and Red Ruffing, whom they traded for one Cedric Durst.

Another case of mistaken calling was that of the young third baseman on the 1933 team. He seemed no more gifted than the rest of that untalented crew, so he was shipped to the Phillies. There he came under the tutelage of player-manager Jimmie Wilson, an outstanding catcher who could recognize a star pitcher in a failed infielder. Perhaps with Bucky Walters pitching for them in 1938, the Red Sox would have finished first instead of second.

Third baseman Marty McManus was attending mass when the Red Sox appointed him skipper. His team would immediately test his capacity for Christian forgiveness. One of the biggest miscreants was good-hit no-field Smead Jolley. With saintly patience manager McManus spent hours showing Smead how to negotiate the incline in front of the left field wall—the famous "Duffy's Cliff." While tracking a fly ball shortly afterward, Smead went up the incline flawlessly and caught the ball, only to fall on his backside coming down and drop the ball.

"For Christ sake!" McManus berated him. "I spent all that time showing you how to go up the cliff and now you muff it."

"Yeah," retorted Jolley, "but you didn't show me how to come down."

Another of McManus' charges was first baseman Dale Alexander, who won the batting title in 1932 playing with two different teams, Detroit and Boston. By 1934, he was out of the majors, testimony to his fielding.

Wes Ferrell—fine at pitching, overrated at checkers.

Pete Jablonowski pitched for the Red Sox in 1933. His record was so bad that he couldn't stay. Absolutely disgusted with himself, he decided to change his name. He came back to the majors as Pete Appleton and posted a 14-6 record with Washington in 1936.

The cloak of modesty did not fit the shoulders of Buck ("Bobo") Newsom. Hoping to embarrass the renowned blabbermouth, coach Tom Daly, an old-time catcher, yelled, "Come on, Bobo, I'll warm you up bare-handed." Daly's hands weren't the same for a month, but he did manage to shut up Newsom for a few days.

Another immodest sort was Wes Ferrell, who would frequently walk into the locker room and declare, "I can lick any man in checkers." The boasting prompted Daly to buy some books on the game, study them thoroughly, and challenge Ferrell. He beat the surprised Wes six straight games, after which Ferrell threw the checkerboard out the window.

On September 27, 1935, Cleveland led Boston 5-3 in the bottom of the ninth, but Boston had the bases loaded, none out, and Joe Cronin at bat. Joe hit a scorching line drive that struck the Indians' third baseman, Odel Hale, in the head. It then caromed to shortstop Billy Knickerbocker, who caught it on the fly and tossed it to Roy Hughes on second

to double off Billy Werber. Hughes then threw to first, trapping Mel Almada. Triple play.

Although Heinie Manush played only one season (1936) with the Sox, he left his mark. A popular movie of the day pictured an actor trying to get to sleep in an upper berth. His method of counting sheep was moaning, "Heinie Manush, Heinie Manush, Heinie Manush . . ." to the rhythm of the grinding train wheels. Thus, whenever Manush would climb into his berth on road trips, the players took up the cry throughout the Pullman. Heinie was flattered but admitted, "I never got much sleep on a train after that."

In 1945, Hal Peck of the Athletics made a wide throw to second base, trying to catch a Red Sox runner. The ball hit one of the many Fenway pigeons "on the wing," killed the poor bird, and was neatly deflected into the hands of the Athletics' second baseman. The runner was tagged out.

Mike Ryba was the epitome of the journeyman ball player. Once in the minors (name any league—Mike was in it) he demonstrated his versatility by playing a different position each inning and, when the game was over, by driving the team bus to the train.

In Fenway he added another number to his act. He became known as "the Colonel of the Bullpen," because he would line up the inhabitants of the warm-up area for the National Anthem, then exchange salutes with them after it was finished.

Whether or not Johnny Pesky held the ball too long as Enos Slaughter raced toward home with the winning run of the 1946 World Series, the critics were quick to condemn him. Realizing that it would be more painful than helpful to attempt to rebut the consensus, the shortstop opted for the therapy of escape. He repaired to his native Oregon and kept his public appearances to a minimum.

In an effort to help the harried shortstop forget baseball, an old friend invited him to attend the Oregon-Oregon State football game. Pesky agreed, and armed with dark glasses to ensure his anonymity, he watched the traditional rivals do battle. It was less than a competently played game. Both teams fumbled the ball away consistently, and as the crowd grew restive, Pesky experienced the luxury of watching somebody else take the heat. Then a loudmouth fan behind him shouted a novel suggestion to the fumbling footballers. "Give the ball to Pesky," he bellowed. "He'll hold on to it."

When Joe McCarthy took over as manager of the Red Sox in 1948, everyone waited for "the Great Necktie Confrontation." When in charge of the Yankees, Marse Joe had insisted with the firmness of a Parris Island drill instructor that all his players wear neckties at meals. It was well known that Ted Williams looked upon the cravat as God's device to punish man for taking Eve's apple. McCarthy settled the issue the first day of spring training by showing up for breakfast with a bright sport shirt, open at the neck. He explained, "The day I can't get along with a four hundred hitter I should quit."

On an opening day at the nation's capital in the fifties, President Eisen-

178

Pumpsie Green, Sox' first black ball player,
chats with the next, Earl Wilson, left. No Jackie
Robinson, Pumpsie ended up with the Mets.

Old adversaries—Slaughter and Pesky—kiss and make up before old-timers' game in 1971, 25 years after fate paired them off in one of baseball's most famous plays.

hower prepared to throw out the first ball. The shrewd Jimmy Piersall waited until Ike had winged it, then dashed over to him while a group of players scuffled to recover the ball. Piersall presented Ike with another ball and pleaded, "Mr. President, would you sign this one while those idiots scramble for that one?" Ike grinned and complied.

Gene Conley, Red Sox pitcher in 1961-63 and also a member of the world champion Boston Celtics, once tried to convince Elijah ("Pumpsie") Green to go to Israel in midseason. Conley actually went to the airport for the trip, but the prophet never showed up.

The Red Sox have had a Hawk (Ken Harrelson), a Grey Eagle (Tris Speaker), a Birdie (George Tebbetts), a Chick (Wilson Fewster), a Duck (Dick Schofield), and now a Rooster (Rick Burleson). They have also had a Big Bill (Dineen), a Long Tom (Winsett), a Pudge (Fisk), a Fatty (Fothergill), a Skinny (Brown), and a Stuffy (McInnis). Finally, they have had a pitcher named Nixon and a catcher named Agnew, who was once arrested in Washington, D.C.

LINESCORE

Red Sox
All-time Roster

A

Adair, Jerry, IF	1967-68
Adams, Bob, P	1925
Agganis, Harry, 1B	1954
Agnew, Sam, C	1916-18
Alexander, Dale, 1B	1932-33
Almada, Mel, OF	1933-36
Altrock, Nick, P	1902-03
Alvarado, Luis, SS-3B	1968-70
Anderson, Spitball, P	1909, 1913
Andres, Ernest, 3B	1946
Andrews, Ivy, P	1932-33
Andrews, Mike, 2B-SS	1966-70
Aparicio, Luis, SS	1971-73
Arellanes, Frank, P	1908-10
Armbruster, Charlie, C	1905-06
Asbjornson, Asby, C	1928-29
Aspromonte, Ken, 2B	1957-58
Atkins, Doc, P	1902
Atkins, Jim, P	1950, 1952
Auker, Eldon, P	1939
Aulds, Doyle, C	1947
Avila, Bobby, 2B	1959
Azcue, Joe, C	1969

B

Bader, Loren, P	1917-18
Bagby, Jim, P	1938-40, 1946
Bailey, Gene, OF	1920
Baker, Al, P	1938
Baker, Floyd, 3B-2B	1953-54
Baker, Tracy, 1B	1911
Ball, Neal, 2B	1912
Barbare, Walter, SS	1918
Barberich, Frank, P	1910
Barna, Babe, OF	1943
Barr, Steve, P	1974
Barrett, Bill, OF	1929-30
Barrett, Bob, 3B	1929
Barrett, Frank, P	1944-45
Barrett, Jimmy, OF	1907-08
Barry, Ed, P	1905-07
Barry, Jack, 2B	1915-17, 1919
Batts, Matt, C	1947-51
Baumann, Frank, P	1955-59
Bayne, Bill, P	1929-30
Bell, Gary, P	1967-68
Beniquez, Juan, SS-OF	1971-72, 1974-
Bennett, Dennis, P	1965-67
Bennett, Frank, P	1927-28
Benton, Al, P	1952
Berberet, Lou, C	1958
Berg, Moe, C	1935-39
Berger, Boz, IF	1939
Berry, Charlie, C	1928-32
Bevan, Hal, 3B	1952
Beville, Chas. E., P	1901
Bigelow, Elliott, OF	1929
Bischoff, Smiley, C	1925-26
Bishop, Max, 2B-1B	1934-35
Black, Dave, P	1923
Blackwell, Tim, C	1974
Blethen, Clarence, P	1923
Bluhm, Harvey, PH	1918
Boerner, Larry, P	1932
Bolin, Bob, P	1970-73
Bolling, Milt, IF	1952-56
Boone, Ray, 1B	1960
Borland, Tom, P	1960-61
Boone, Ike, OF	1923-25
Boudreau, Lou, SS-3B	1951-52

Bowers, Stew, P	1935-37
Bowman, Joe, P	1944-45
Bowsfield, Ted, P	1958-60
Bradley, Herb, P	1927-29
Bradley, Hugh, 1B	1910-12
Brady, Cliff, 2B	1920
Brady, King, P	1908
Brandon, Darrell, P	1966-68
Bratchi, Fred, OF	1926-27
Bressoud, Eddie, SS	1962-65
Brett, Ken, P	1967, 1969-71
Brewer, Tom, P	1954-61
Brickner, Ralph, P	1952
Brillheart, Jim, P	1931
Brodowski, Dick, P	1952, 1955
Brown, Hal, P	1953-54
Brown, Lloyd, P	1933
Brown, Mace, P	1942-43, 1946
Bucher, Jim, 3B-2B	1944-45
Buddin, Don, SS	1956, 1958-61
Burchell, Fred, P	1907-09
Burda, Bob, 1B	1972
Burkett, Jess, OF	1905
Burleson, Rick, OF-IF	1974
Burns, George, 1B	1922-23
Busby, Jim, OF	1959-60
Bush, Bullet Joe, P	1918-21
Bushelman, Jack, P	1911-12
Bushey, Frank, P	1927, 1930
Butland, Bill, P	1940, 1942, 1946-47
Byerly, Bud, P	1958-60

C

Cady, Hick, C	1912-17
Caldwell, Earl, P	1948
Caldwell, Ray, P	1919
Camilli, Dolph, 1B	1945
Campbell, Paul, 1B-OF	1941-42, 1946
Carbo, Bernie, OF-IF	1974
Carey, Tom, IF	1939-42, 1946
Carlisle, Rosy, OF	1908
Carlston, Swede, SS	1911
Carlyle, Cleo, OF	1927
Carlyle, Dizzy, OF	1925-26
Carrigan, Bill, C	1906, 1908-16
Carroll, Ed, P	1929
Casale, Jerry, P	1958-60
Cascarella, Joe, P	1935-36
Cater, Danny, 1B-3B	1972-
Cecil, Rex, P	1944-45
Cepeda, Orlando, DH	1973
Chadbourne, Chet, 2B-OF	1906-07
Chakales, Bob, P	1957
Chaney, Esty, P	1913
Chapin, Ed, C	1920-22
Chapman, Ben, OF	1937-38
Charton, Frank, P	1964
Chase, Ken, P	1942-43
Chech, Charlie, P	1909
Chesbro, Jack, P	1909
Chittum, Nelson, P	1959-60
Christopher, Joe, OF	1966
Christopher, Lloyd, OF	1945
Cicero, Joe, OF	1929-30
Cicotte, Eddie, P	1908-12
Cisco, Galen, P	1961-62, 1968
Cissell, Bill, 2B	1934
Clark, Danny, 3B	1924
Clarke, Otie, P	1945
Clemons, Lance, P	1974
Cleveland, Reggie, P	1974

182

Clevenger, Truman, P 1954
Clinton, Lou, OF 1960-64
Clowers, Bill, P 1926
Cochran, George, 3B 1918
Coffey, Jack, 2B 1918
Collins, Harry, OF 1922
Collins, Jimmy, 3B 1901-07
Collins, Ray, P 1909-15
Collins, Shano, OF-1B 1921-25
Combs, Merrill, 3B 1947, 1949-50
Comstock, Ralph, P 1915
Conley, Gene, P 1961-63
Congalton, Bunk, OF 1907
Conigliaro, Billy, OF 1969-71
Conigliaro, Tony, 1B 1964-67, 1969-70
Connally, Bud, SS 1925
Connolly, Ed, C 1929-32
Connolly, Ed, P 1964
Connolly, Joe, OF 1924
Conroy, Bill, C 1942-44
Consolo, Billy, OF 1953-59
Cooke, Dusty, OF 1933-36
Cooney, Scoops, 2B 1917
Cooper, Cecil, 1B-OF 1970-
Cooper, Guy, P 1915
Correll, Vic, C 1972
Coughtry, Marlan, 2B 1960
Coumbe, Fritz, P 1914
Cramer, Doc, OF 1936-40
Cravath, Gavvy, OF 1908
Creeden, Pat, 2B 1931
Cremins, Bob, P 1927
Criger, Lou, C 1901-08
Cronin, Joe, SS-IF 1935-45
Culberson, Leon, OF 1943-47
Culp, Ray, P 1968-71
Cuppy, Nig, P 1901
Curtis, John, P 1970-73

D
Dahlgren, Babe, 1B 1935-36
Daley, Pete, C 1955-59
Dallessandro, Dom, OF 1937
Danzig, Babe, 1B 1909
Daughters, Red, PH 1937
Deal, Cot, P 1947-48
Deininger, Pep, P 1902
Delock, Ike, P 1952-53, 1955-62
Demeter, Don, OF 1966-67
Dente, Sam, 3B 1947
Derrick, Jim, OF 1970
Desautels, Gene, C 1937-40
Deutsch, Mel, P 1946
Devine, Mickey, C 1920
DeViney, Hal, P 1920
De Vormer, Al, C 1923
Dickey, George, C 1935-36
Dickman, Emerson, P 1936-41
Dimaggio, Dom, OF 1940-42, 1946-53
Dinneen, Big Bill, P 1902-07
Di Pietro, Bob, OF 1951
Dobens, Ray, P 1929
Dobson, Joe, P 1941-43, 1946-50, 1954
Dodge, Sam, P 1921-22
Doerr, Bobby, 2B 1937-51
Donahue, Jiggs, OF 1923
Donahue, Pat, C 1908-09
Donohue, Pete, P 1932
Doran, Tom, C 1904-06
Dorish, Harry, P 1947-49
Dougherty, Patsy, OF 1902-04

Dowd, Tommy, OF 1901
Doyle, Howard, C 1943
Drago, Dick, P 1974
Dreisewerd, Clem, P 1944-46
Dropo, Walt, 1B 1949-52
Dubuc, Jean, P 1918
Dugan, Jumping Joe, 3B 1922
Duliba, Bob, P 1965
Dumont, George, P 1919
Durham, Bull, P 1929-32
Durst, Cedric, OF 1930

E
Earley, Arnie, P 1960-65
Eggert, Elmer, 2B 1927
Ehmke, Howard, P 1923-26
Eibel, Hack, P 1920
Ellsworth, Dick, P 1968-69
Engle, Clyde, OF-IF 1910-14
Evans Al, C 1951
Evans, Bill, P 1951
Evans, Dewey, OF 1972
Evers, Hoot, OF 1952-54
Ezzell, Homer, 3B-SS 1924-25

F
Fanzone, Carmen, 3B 1970
Farrell, Doc, 2B 1935
Farrell, Duke, C 1903-05
Ferguson, Alex, P 1922-25
Ferrell, Rick, C 1933-37
Ferrell, Wes, P 1934-37
Ferris, Hobe, 2B 1901-07
Ferriss, Boo, P 1945-50
Fewster, Chick, OF-IF 1922-23
Fine, Tom, P 1947
Finney, Lou, OF-1B 1939-42, 1944-45
Fiore, Mike, 1B 1970-71
Fischer, Hank, P 1966-67
Fisk, Carlton, C 1969, 1971-
Fitzgerald, Howard, OF 1926
Flagstead, Ira, OF 1923-29
Flair, Al, 1B 1941
Fleming, Bill, P 1940-41
Flowers, Ben, P 1951, 1953
Foreman, Frank, P 1901
Foreman, Happy, P 1926
Fornieles, Mike, P 1957-63
Fortune, Gary, P 1920
Foster, Kid, 3B-2B 1920-22
Foster, Rube, P 1913-17
Fothergill, Fatty, OF 1933
Fowler, Boob, 3B 1962
Fox, Pete, OF 1941-45
Foxx, Jimmy, 1B-C-3B 1936-42
Francis, Ray, P 1925
Freeman, Buck, OF-1B 1901-07
Freeman, Hersh, P 1952-54
Freeman, John, OF 1927
French, Charlie, 2B-SS-OF 1901-10
Friend, Owen, IF 1955
Foy, Joe, 3B-SS 1966-68
Fuhr, Oscar, P 1924-25
Fuller, Frank, 2B 1923
Fullerton, Curt, P 1921-25, 1933

G
Gaffke, Fabian, OF 1936-39
Gagliano, Phil, OF-IF 1971-72
Gainor, Del, 1B-OF 1914-17, 1919
Galehouse, Denny, P 1939-40, 1947-49

Gallagher, Bob, PH	1972	Hash, Herb, P	1940-41
Gallagher, Ed, P	1932	Hatfield, Fred, SS-3B	1950-52
Galvin, Jim, PH	1930	Hatton, Grady, 3B	1954-56
Garback, Bob, C	1945	Hausmann, Clem, P	1944-45
Gardner, Billy, IF	1962-63	Hayden, Jack, OF	1906
Gardner, Larry, 3B-2B	1908-17	Hayes, Frank, C	1947
Garman, Mike, P	1969, 1971-73	Hearn, Ed, SS	1910
Garrison, Cliff, P	1928	Heffner, Bob, P	1962-65
Garrison, Ford, OF	1943-44	Heflin, Randy, P	1945-46
Gaston, Alex, C	1926-27	Heimach, Lefty, P	1926
Gaston, Milt, P	1929-31	Hemphill, Charlie, OF	1901
Geiger, Gary, OF	1959-65	Hendryx, Tim, OF	1920-21
Gelbert, Charlie, IF	1940	Henricksen, Swede, OF	1911-17
Gerber, Wally, SS	1928-29	Henry, Bill, P	1952-55
Gernert, Dick, 1B	1952-59	Henry, Jim, P	1936-37
Gessler, Doc, OF	1908-09	Herrara, Mike, IF	1925-26
Geyan, Chappie, SS	1924-25	Herrin, Tom, P	1954
Giannini, Joe, SS	1911	Heving, Joe, P	1938-40
Gibson, Norwood, P	1903-06	Heving, John, C	1924-25, 1928-30
Gibson, Russ, C	1967-69	Hickman, Charlie, 1B	1902
Gilbert, Andy, OF	1942-1946	Higgins, Pinky, 3B	1937-38, 1946
Gile, Don, 1B-OF	1959-62	Hiller, Hob, IF	1920-21
Gilhooley, Frank, OF	1919	Hillman, Dave, P	1960-61
Gillespie, Bob, P	1950	Hinkle, Gordie, C	1934
Gillis, Grant, 2B	1929	Hinrichs, Paul, P	1951
Ginsberg, Myron, C	1961	Hinson, Paul, PH	1928
Glaze, Ralph, P	1906-08	Hismer, Harley, P	1951
Gleason, Harry, 3B-OF	1903	Hitchcock, Bill, IF	1948-50
Glenn, Joe, C	1940	Hoblitzel, Dick, 1B	1914-18
Godwin, John, IF-OF	1905-06	Hockette, George, P	1934-35
Gonzales, Eusebio, SS	1918	Hodapp, John, 2B	1933
Gonzales, Joe, P	1937	Hoderlein, Mel, 3B-2B	1951
Gooch, Johnny, C	1933	Hoeft, Billy, P	1959
Goodman, Billy	1947-56	Hoey, John, OF	1906-08
Gosger, Jim, OF	1962, 1965-66	Holcombe, Ken, P	1953
Graham, Art, OF	1934-35	Hofmann, Fred, C	1927-28
Graham, Charlie, C	1906	Holm, Bill, C	1945
Gray, Dave, P	1964	Hooper, Harry, OF	1909-20
Green, Lenny, OF	1965-66	Horton, Tony, OF-1B	1964-67
Green, Pumpsie, SS-2B	1959-62	Howard, Elston, C	1967-68
Gregg, Vern, P	1914-16	Howard, Paul, OF	1909
Griffin, Doug, 2B	1971-	Howe, Les, P	1923-24
Griffin, Marty, P	1928	Hoyt, Waite, P	1919-20
Grilli, Guido, P	1966	Hudson, Sid, P	1952-54
Grimes, Ray, 1B	1920	Hughes, Ed, P	1905-06
Grimshaw, Moose, 1B-OF	1905-07	Hughes, Terry, 3B	1974-
Grissom, Marv, P	1953	Hughes, Tom, P	1902-03
Gross, Ewell, SS	1925	Hughson, Tex, P	1941-44, 1946-49
Grove, Lefty, P	1934-41	Humphreys, Bill, P	1938
Guerra, Mike, C	1951	Hunt, Ben, P	1910
Guerrero, Mario, SS-2B	1973-	Hunter, Buddy, IF	1971, 1973
Guindon, Bob, OF	1964	Hunter, Herb, OF	1920
Gumpert, Randy, P	1952	Hurd, Tom, P	1954-56
Gunning, Hy, 1B	1911	Hustings, Bert, P	1901
Gutteridge, Don, 2B-3B	1946-47		

H

J

Hageman, Casey, P	1911-12	Jablonowski, Pete, P	1932
Haley, Ray, C	1915-16	Jackson, Ron, 1B	1960
Hall, Sea Lion, P	1909-13	Jacobson, Baby Doll, OF	1926-27
Haney, Fred, 3B	1926-27	Jacobson, Beany, P	1907
Hardy, Carrol, OF	1960-62	Jamerson, Charlie, P	1924
Harper, Harry, P	1920	James, Bill, P	1919
Harper, Tommy, OF	1972-	Janvrin, Hal, IF	1911-17
Harrell, Billy, IF	1961	Jarvis, Ray, P	1969-70
Harrelson, Ken, 1B-OF	1967-69	Jenkins, Tom, OF	1925
Harris, Joe, P	1905-07	Jensen, Jackie, OF	1954-61
Harris, Joe, 1B-OF	1922-25	Johnson, Adam, P	1914
Harris, Mickey, P	1940-41, 1946-49	Johnson, Bob, OF	1932-35
Harriss, Bill, P	1938	Johnson, Bob, OF	1944-45
Harriss, Slim, P	1926-27	Johnson, Henry, P	1933-35
Harshman, Jack, P	1959	Johnson, Vic, P	1944-45
Hartenstein, Chuck, P	1970	Johnson, Earl, P	1940-41, 1946-50
Hartley, Slick, C	1927	Jolley, Smead, OF	1932-33
Hartman, Charlie, P	1908	Jones, Carlie C., OF	1901
Hash, Bad News, 2B	1941	Jones, Dalton, IF	1964-69
		Jones, Jake, 1B	1947-48

Jones, Sad Sam, P	1916-21
Joost, Eddie, IF	1955
Josephson, Duane, C	1971-72
Judd, Oscar, P	1941-45
Judge, Joe, 1B	1933-34

K

Kallio, Rudy, P	1925
Karger, Ed, P	1909-11
Karl, Andy, P	1943
Karow, Marty, IF	1927
Karr, Benn, P	1920-22
Kasko, Eddie, IF	1966
Kell, George, 3B	1952-54
Kellet, Al, P	1924
Kellet, Red, IF	1934
Kelly, Ed, P	1914
Keltner, Ken, 3B	1950
Kemmerer, Russ, P	1954-55, 1957
Kennedy, Bill, P	1953
Kennedy, John, IF	1970-74
Keough, Marty, OF	1956-60
Kiefer, Joe, P	1925-26
Kiely, Leo, P	1951, 1954-56, 1958-59
Killilay, Jack, P	1911
Kinder, Ellis, P	1948-55
Kinney, Walt, P	1918
Klaus, Billy, IF	1955-58
Kleinow, Red, C	1910-11
Kline, Bob, P	1930-33
Kline, Ron, P	1969
Klinger, Bob, P	1946-47
Knight, John, 3B	1907
Kolstad, Hal, P	1962-63
Koonce, Cal, P	1970-71
Kosco, Andy, OF	1972
Kramer, Jack, P	1948-49
Krausse, Lou, P	1972-73
Kroh, Rube, P	1906-07
Kellum, Win, P	1901
Kroner, John, IF	1935-36
Krug, Marty, SS	1912

L

LaChance, Candy, 1B	1902-05
LaForest, Ty, 3B-OF	1945
Lahoud, Joe, OF	1968-71
Lake, Eddie, SS	1943-45
Lamabe, Jack, P	1963-65
Lamar, Bill, OF	1919
Landis, Bill, P	1967-69
Landis, Jim, OF	1967
Langford, Sam, PH	1926
LaPorte, Frank, 2B-OF	1908
Lary, Lyn, SS	1934
Lazor, John, OF	1943-46
Lee, Bill, P	1969-
Lee, Dud, SS	1924-26
LeFebvre, Bill, P	1938-39
Legett, Lou, C	1933-35
Leheney, Regis, P	1932
Leibold, Nemo, OF	1921
Lenhardt, Don, OF	1952
Leonard, Dutch, P	1913-18
Lepcio, Ted, IF	1952-59
Lerchem, Dutch, SS	1910
LeRoy, Louis, P	1910
Lewis, Duffy, OF	1910-17
Lewis, John, 2B	1911
Lewis, Ted, P	1901
Lipon, Johnny, SS-3B	1952-53
Lisenbee, Hod, P	1929-32
Littlefield, Dick, P	1950
Lock, Don, OF	1969
Loepp, George, OF	1928
Lonborg, Jim, P	1965-71

Lonergan, Walt, 2B	1911
Lord, Harry, 3B	1907-10
Lucas, John, OF	1931-32
Lucey, Joe, P	1925
Lucier, Lou, P	1943-44
Lundgren, Del, P	1926-27
Lupien, Tony, 1B	1940, 1942-43
Lyle, Sparky, P	1967-71
Lynch, Walt, C	1922
Lynn, Fred, OF	1974

M

MacFayden, Danny, P	1926-32
MacLeod, Bill, P	1962
Madden, Tom, C	1909-11
Magrini, Pete, P	1966
Mahoney, Chris, P-OF	1910
Mahoney, Jim, SS	1959
Mallett, Gene, OF	1959
Maloy, Paul, P	1913
Malzone, Frank, 3B	1955-65
Mantilla, Felix, OF-IF	1963-65
Manush, Heinie, OF	1936
Marchildon, Phil, P	1950
Marcum, John, P	1936-38
Marichal, Juan, P	1974
Marquardt, Ollie, 2B	1931
Marshall, Bill, PH	1931
Martin, Babe, C	1948-49
Masterson, Walt, P	1949-52
Matchik, Tommy, 3B	1970
Mathews, Bill, P	1909
Mauch, Gene, 2B	1956-57
Maxwell, Charlie, OF	1950-54
Maynard, Chick, SS	1922
Mays, Carl, P	1915-18
McAuliffe, Dick, 2B-3B	1974
McBride, Tom, OF-1B	1943-47
McCabe, Dick, P	1918
McCall, John, P	1948-49
McCann, Bob, SS	1926
McCarver, Tim, C	1974
McConnell, Amby, 2B	1908-10
McDermott, Mickey, P	1948-53
McDonald, Jim, P	1950
McFarland, Ed, C	1908
McGah, Ed, C	1946-47
McGlothen, Lynn, P	1972-73
McGovern, Art, C	1905
McGraw, Bob, P	1919
McGuire, Deacon, C	1907-08
McHale, Jim, OF	1908
McHale, Marty, P	1910-11, 1916
McInnis, Stuffy, 1B	1918-21
McKain, Archie, P	1937-38
McLaughlin, Jud, P	1931-33
McLean, Larry, 1B	1901
McMahon, Doc, P	1908
McMahon, Don, P	1966-67
McManus, Marty, IF	1931-33
McMillan, Norm, 3B	1923
McNair, Eric, IF	1936-38
McNally, Mike, IF	1915-17, 1919-20
McNaughton, Gordon, P	1932
McNeil, Norm, C	1919
McWilliams, Bill, P	1931
Mejias, Roman, OF	1963-64
Mele, Sam, OF	1947-49, 1954-55
Melillo, Oscar, 2B	1935-37
Menosky, Mike, OF	1920-23
Meola, Mike, P	1933, 1936
Merena, Spike, P	1934
Merson, Jack, 2B	1953
Metkovich, George, OF-1B	1943-46
Meyer, Russ, P	1957
Midkiff, Dick, P	1938

Miles, Dee 1943
Miller, Bing, OF 1935-36
Miller, Elmer, OF 1922
Miller, Hack, OF 1918
Miller, Otto, IF 1930-32
Miller, Rick, OF 1971-
Mills, Buster, OF 1937
Mills, Dick, P 1970
Minarcin, Rudy, P 1956-57
Mitchell, Fred, P 1901-02
Mitchell, Johnny, SS 1922-23
Moford, Herb, P 1959
Molyneaux, Vince, P 1918
Momcewicz, Fred, SS 1928
Monbouquette, Bill, P 1958-65
Montgomery, Bob, C 1970-
Moore, Bill, C 1926-27
Moore, Wiley, P 1931-32
Morehead, Dave, P 1963-68
Moret, Rogelio, P 1970-
Morgan, Cy, P 1907-09
Morgan, Ed, 1B 1934
Morgan, Jim, 3B 1906
Morris, Ed, P 1928-31
Morrissey, Deacon, P 1901
Morton, Guy, PH 1954
Mosely, Earl, P 1913
Moser, Walt, P 1911
Moses, Gerry, C 1965, 1968-70
Moses, Wally, OF 1946-48
Moskiman, Doc, OF 1910
Moss, Les, C 1951
Mueller, Gordy, P 1950
Muffett, Billy, P 1960-62
Mulleavy, Greg, PH 1933
Muller, Fred, 2B 1933-34
Mulligan, Joe, P 1934
Mulroney, Frank, P 1930
Mundy, Bill, 1B 1913
Murphy, John, P 1947
Murphy, Walter, P 1931
Murray, George, P 1923-24
Muser, Tony, 1B 1969
Musser, Paul, P 1919
Mustaikis, Alex, P 1940
Myer, Buddy, IF 1927-28
Myers, Elmer, P 1920
Myers, Ralph Hap, 1B 1910-11

N
Nagle, Judge, P 1911
Nagy, Mike, P 1969-72
Narleski, Bill, IF 1929
Neubauer, Hal, P 1925
Neuhause, Don, P 1971-74
Newsome, Buck, P 1937
Newsome, Dick, P 1941-43
Newsome, Skeeter, IF 1941-45
Niarhos, Gus, C 1952-53
Nichols, Chet, P 1960-63
Niemiec, Al, 2B 1934
Nietzke, Ernest, P 1921
Niles, Harry, OF-2B 1908-10
Nippert, Merlin, P 1962
Nixon, Russ, C 1960-65, 1968
Nixon, Willard, P 1950-58
Nonnenkamp, Leo, OF 1938-40
Nourse, Chet, P 1909
Nunamaker, Les, C 1911-14

O
Oberlin, Frank, P 1906-07
O'Brien, Bucky, P 1911-13
O'Brien, Jack, OF-3B 1903
O'Brien, Sydney, IF 1969

O'Brien, Tommy, OF 1949-50
O'Doul, Lefty, P 1923
Oglivie, Ben, OF 1971-73
Okrie, Len, C 1952
Oliver, Gene, C-1B 1968
Oliver, Tom, OF 1930-33
Olmstead, Hank, P 1905
Olsen, Al, PH 1943
Olson, Karl, OF 1951, 1953-55
Olson, Marv, 1B 1931-32
Olson, Ted, P 1936-38
O'Neill, Bill, OF 1904
O'Neill, Emmett, P 1943-45
O'Neill, Steve, C 1924
Orme, George, P 1920
O'Rourke, Blackie, SS-3B 1922
Osinski, Dan, P 1966-67
Ostdiek, Harry, C 1908
Ostermueller, Fritz, P 1934-40
Ostrowski, John, PH 1948
Owen, Marvin, 3B-1B 1940
Owen, Mickey, C 1954
Owens, Frank, C 1905

P
Pagliarone, Jim, C 1955, 1960-62
Palm, Mike, P 1948
Papai, Al, P 1950
Pape, Larry, P 1909-11
Parent, Fred, SS 1901-07
Parnell, Mel, P 1947-56
Partee, Roy, C 1943-44, 1946-47
Partenheimer, Stan, P 1944
Pascal, Ben, OF 1920
Patten, Case, P 1908
Patterson, Hank, C 1932
Pattin, Marty, P 1972-73
Pavletich, Don, 1B-C 1970-71
Peacock, John, C 1937-44
Pellagrini, Eddie, 3B-2B 1946-47
Pennock, Herb, P 1915-22, 1934
Perrin, John, OF 1921
Pertica, Bill, P 1918
Pesky, John, IF 1942, 1946-52
Peters, Gary, P 1970-72
Peterson, Bob, C 1906-07
Petrocelli, Rico, SS-3B 1963, 1965
Philley, Dave, OF 1962
Phillips, Norm, P 1970
Picinich, Val, C 1923-25
Pickering, Urbane, 2B-3B 1931-32
Piercy, Bill, P 1921-24
Piersall, Jim, OF 1950-58
Pipgras, George, P 1933-35
Pittinger, Pinky, OF-IF 1921-23
Pizarro, Juan, P 1968-69
Plews, Herb, PH 1959
Poindexter, Jinx, P 1936
Pole, Dick, P 1973-74
Polly, Nick, 3B 1945
Pond, Ralph, OF 1910
Porter, Dick, OF 1934
Porterfield, Bob, P 1956-58
Potter, Nelson, P 1941
Poulsen, Ken, SS 1967
Pratt, Del, 2B 1921-22
Pratt, Larry, C 1914
Prothro, Doc, 3B 1925
Pruiett, Tex, P 1907-08
Purtell, Billy, SS 1910-11
Pytlack, Frank, C 1941, 1945-46

Q
Quinn, Frank, P 1949-50
Quinn, John, P 1922-25

R

Radatz, Dick, P	1962-66
Reder, John, 1B	1932
Reeves, Bob, IF	1929-31
Regan, Bill, 2B	1926-30
Rehg, Wally, OF	1913-15
Reichle, Dick, OF	1922-23
Renna, Bill, OF	1958-59
Repulski, Rip, OF	1960-61
Reynolds, Carl, OF	1934-35
Rhyne, Hall, SS	1929-32
Rhodes, Gordon, P	1932-35
Rice, Jim, OF	1974
Rich, Woody, P	1939-41
Richter, Al, SS	1951, 1953
Riggert, Joe, OF	1911
Rigney, Topper, SS	1926-27
Ripley, Walt, P	1935
Rising, Perry, OF	1905
Robinson, Aaron, C	1951
Robinson, Floyd, OF	1968
Robinson, Jack, P	1949
Rodgers, Bill, 2B	1915
Rogell, Billy, IF-OF	1925, 1927-28
Rogers, Lee, P	1938
Roggenburk, Garry, P	1966, 1968-69
Rohr, Bill, P	1967
Rollings, Red, IF	1927-28
Romo, Vincente, P	1970-71
Rosar, Buddy, C	1950-51
Rosenthal, Si, OF	1925-26
Ross, Buster, P	1924-26
Roth, Braggo, OF	1919
Rothrock, Jack, OF	1925-32
Ruel, Muddy, C	1921-22, 1931
Ruffing, Red, P	1924-30
Runnels, Pete, IF	1958-62
Russell, Allan, P	1919-22
Russell, Jack, P	1926-32, 1936
Russell, Rip, 3B-2B	1946-47
Ruth, Babe, P-OF	1914-19
Ryan, Jack, P	1909
Ryan, John, OF	1929
Ryan, Mike, C	1964-67
Ryba, Mike, P-C	1941-46
Rye, Gene, OF	1931

S

Sadowski, Bob, P	1966
Sadowski, Ed, C	1960
Sanders, Ken, P	1966
Santiago, Jose, P	1966
Satriano, Tom, C-IF	1969-70
Sayles, Bill, P	1939
Scarborough, Ray, P	1951-52
Scarrit, Russ, OF	1929-31
Schang, Wally, C	1918-20
Schanz, Charley, P	1950
Scherbarth, Bob, C	1950
Schilling, Chuck, 2B	1961-65
Schlesinger, Rudy, PH	1965
Schlitzer, Biff, P	1909
Schmee, George, P-1B-OF	1952
Schmitz, John, P	1956
Schofield, Dick, IF	1969-70
Schreckengost, Ossee, C	1901
Schroll, Al, P	1958-59
Schwall, Don, P	1961-62
Scott, Everett, SS	1914-21
Scott, George, 1B-3B	1966-71
Seeds, Bob, 1B-OF	1933-34
Segui, Diego, P	1974
Selback, Kip, OF	1904-05
Settlemire, Lefty, P	1928
Shaner, Wally, OF	1926-27
Shanks, Hank, IF-OF	1923-24

Shannon, Red, 2B	1919
Shaw, Al, C	1907
Shea, John, P	1928
Shea, Merv, C	1933
Shean, Dave, 2B	1918
Sheldon, Ron, P	1966
Sheridan, Neill, PH	1948
Shields, Ben, P	1930
Shofner, Strick, 3B	1947
Shore, Ernie, P	1914-17
Short, Bill, P	1966
Shorten, Chick, OF	1915-17
Siebern, Norm, OF-IF	1967-68
Siebert, Sonny, P	1969-73
Simmons, Al, OF	1943
Simmons, Pat, P	1928-29
Sisler, George, P	1956-59
Skinner, Camp, P	1923
Skok, Craig, P	1973
Slattery, Jack, C	1901
Slayton, Steve, P	1928
Snall, Charlie, P	1930
Smith, Al, OF	1964
Smith, Alec, C	1903
Smith, Bob, P	1955
Smith, Charlie, P	1909-11
Smith, Doug, P	1912
Smith, Edgar, P	1947
Smith, Elmer, OF	1921
Smith, Frank, P	1910-11
Smith, George, P	1930
Smith, George, 2B-SS	1966
Smith, John, 1B	1931
Smith, Paddy, C	1920
Smith, Pete, P	1962-63
Smith, Reggie, OF-2B	1966-73
Snell, Wally, C	1913
Solters, Moose, OF	1934-35
Sothoron, Allen, P	1921
Spanswick, Bill, P	1964
Spence, Stan, OF	1940-41, 1948-49
Spognardi, Andy, IF	1932
Spring, Jack, P	1957
Stallard, Tracy, P	1960-62
Sommers, Rudy, P	1926-27
Sparks, Tully, P	1902
Speaker, Tris, OF	1907-15
Spencer, Tubby, C	1909
Stahl, Chick, OF	1901-06
Stahl, Jake, 1B-OF-C	1903, 1908-10, 1912-13
Standert, Jerry, 1B	1929
Stange, Lee, P	1966-70
Stansbury, John, 3B	1918
Statz, Jigger, OF	1920
Steele, Elmer, P	1907-09
Steiner, Ben, 2B	1945-46
Steiner, Red, C	1945
Stephens, Gene, OF	1952-60
Stephens, Vern, 3B-SS	1948-52
Stephenson, Gerry, P	1963, 1965-68
Stigman, Dick, P	1966
Stimson, Carl, P	1923
Stobbs, Chuck, P	1947-51
Stokes, Al, C	1925-26
Stone, Dean, P	1957
Stone, George, PH	1903
Storie, Howie, C	1931-32
Stringer, Lou, IF	1948-49
Strunk, Amos, 2B	1918
Stuart, Dick, 1B	1963-64
Stumpf, George, OF	1931-33
Sturdivant, Tom, P	1960
Suchecki, Jim, P	1950
Sullivan, Denny, OF	1907-08
Sullivan, Frank, P	1953-60

Sullivan, Haywood, C	1955, 1957, 1959-60	Wambsganss, Bill, 2B	1924-25
		Wanninger, Pee Wee, SS	1927
Summer, Carl, OF	1928	Warner, John, C	1902
Susce, George, P	1955, 1956-58	Warstler, Rabbit, SS-2B	1930-33
Swanson, Bill, IF	1914	Waslewski, Gary, P	1967-68
Sweeney, Bill, 1B	1930-31	Watwood, John, OF	1932-33
Swormstedt, Len, P	1906	Weaver, Monty, P	1939
		Webb, Earl, OF	1930-32
		Webster, Ray, 2B	1960
T		Weiland, Bob, P	1932-34
Tabor, Jim, 3B	1938-44	Welch, Herb, SS	1925
Taitt, Poco, OF	1928, 1929	Welch, John, P	1932-36
Tannehill, Jesse, P	1904-08	Welzer, Tony, P	1926-27
Tarbert, Arlie, OF	1927, 1928	Wenz, Fred, P	1968-69
Tartabull, Jose, OF	1966-68	Werber, Billy, 3B-SS-OF	1933-36
Tasby, Willie, OF	1960	Werle, Bill, P	1953-54
Tate, Ben, C	1932	Wertz, Vic, 1B	1959-61
Tatum, Ken, P	1971-73	White, Sammy, C	1951-59
Taylor, Harry, P	1950-52	Whiteman, George, OF	1907, 1918
Tebbetts, Birdie, C	1947-50	Widmar, Al, P	1947
Terry, Yank, P	1940, 1942-45	Wight, Bill, P	1951-52
Thielman, Jake, P	1908	Wilber, Del, C	1952-54
Thomas, Blaine, P	1911	Wilhoit, Joe, OF	1919
Thomas, Fred, 3B	1918	Williams, Dave, P	1902
Thomas, George, OF-IF	1966-71	Williams, Denny, OF	1924-25, 1928
Thomas, Lee, 1B-OF	1964-65	Williams, Dib, IF	1935
Thomas, Pinch, C	1912-17	Williams, Dick, IF-OF	1963-64
Thomas, Tommy, P	1937	Williams, Ken, OF	1928-29
Thompson, Bobby, OF	1960	Williams, Rip, 1B-C	1911
Thoney, Jack, OF	1908-09, 1911	Williams, Stan, P	1972
Thormahlen, Lefty, P	1921	Williams, Ted, OF	1939-42, 1946-60
Throneberry, Faye, OF	1952, 1955-57	Wills, Ted, P	1959-62
Tiant, Luis, P	1971-	Wilson, Duane, P	1958
Tillman, Bob, C	1962-67	Wilson, Earl, P	1959-66
Tobin, Jack, 3B	1945	Wilson, Gary, 2B	1902
Tobin, John, OF	1926-27	Wilson, George, P	1901-02
Todt, Phil, 1B	1924-30	Wilson, Jack, P	1935-41
Tonneman, Tony, C	1911	Wilson, Jim, P	1945-46
Trimble, Joe, P	1955	Wilson, John, P	1927-28
Trout, Dizzy, P	1952	Wilson, Les, OF	1911
Truesdale, Frank, 2B	1918	Wilson, Squanto, 1B	1914
Turley, Bob, P	1963	Wiltse, Hal, P	1926-28
		Wingfield, Ted, P	1924-27
		Winn, George, P	1919
U		Winsett, Tom, OF	1930-31, 1933
Umphlett, Tom, OF	1953	Winter, George, P	1901-08
Unglaub, Bob, 1B-2B	1907-08	Winters, Clarence, P	1924
		Wise, Rick, P	1974
		Wittig, John, P	1949
V		Wolter, Harry, OF	1909
Van Camp, Al, 1B-OF	1931-32	Wood, Joe, P	1908-15
Vache, Tex, OF	1925	Wood, Joe, P	1944
Vandenberg, Hy, P	1935	Wood, Ken, OF	1952
Veach, Bob, OF	1924-25	Wood, Wilbur, P	1961-64
Veale, Bob, P	1972-	Woods, George, P	1942-45
Vernon, Mickey, 1B	1956-57	Woods, John, P	1924
Vick, Sammy, OF	1921	Workman, Hoge, P	1924
Vitt, Ossie, 3B	1919-21	Worthington, Al, P	1960
Vollmer, Clyde, OF	1950-53	Wright, Tom, OF	1948-51
Volz, Jake, P	1901	Wyatt, John, P	1966-68
Vosmik, Joe, OF	1938-39	Wyckoff, John, P	1916-18
W		**Y**	
Wade, Jake, P	1939	Yastrzemski, Carl, OF-1B	1961-
Wagner, Charlie, P	1938-42, 1946	Yerkes, Steve, SS-2B	1909, 1911-14
Wagner, Gary, P	1969-70	York, Rudy, 1B	1946-47
Wagner, Hal, C	1944, 1946-47	Young, Cy, P	1901-08
Wagner, Heinie, SS-2B	1906-13, 1914-16		
Walberg, Rube, P	1934-37	**Z**	
Walker, Tilly, OF	1916-17	Zahniser, Paul, P	1925-26
Wall, Murray, P	1957-59	Zarilla, Al, OF	1949-50, 1952-53
Walsh, Jimmy, OF	1916-17	Zauchin, Norm, 1B	1951, 1955-57
Walters, Bucky, 3B	1933-34	Zeiser, Matt, P	1914
Walters, Fred, C	1945	Zuber, Bill, P	1946-47
Walters, Roxy, C	1919-23		

Red Sox Year-by-year Standings

Year	Pos	W-L	Pct	GA/GB
1901	2	79-57	.581	4
1902	3	77-60	.562	6½
1903	1	91-47	.659	+14½
1904	1	95-59	.617	+ 1½
1905	4	78-74	.513	16
1906	8	49-105	.318	45½
1907	7	59-90	.396	32½
1908	5	75-79	.487	15½
1909	3	88-63	.583	9½
1910	4	81-72	.529	22½
1911	5	78-75	.510	24
1912	1	105-47	.691	+14
1913	4	79-71	.527	15½
1914	2	91-62	.595	8½
1915	1	101-50	.669	+ 2½
1916	1	91-63	.591	+ 2
1917	2	90-62	.592	9
1918	1	75-51	.595	+ 2½
1919	6	66-71	.482	20½
1920	5	72-81	.471	25½
1921	5	75-79	.487	23½
1922	8	61-93	.396	33
1923	8	61-91	.401	37
1924	7	67-87	.435	25
1925	8	47-105	.309	49½
1926	8	46-107	.301	44½
1927	8	51-103	.331	59
1928	8	57-96	.373	43½
1929	8	58-96	.377	48
1930	8	52-102	.338	50
1931	6	62-90	.408	45
1932	8	43-111	.279	64
1933	7	63-86	.423	34½
1934	4	76-76	.500	24
1935	4	78-75	.510	16
1936	6	74-80	.481	28½
1937	5	80-72	.526	31
1938	2	88-61	.591	9½
1939	2	89-62	.589	17
1940	4	82-72	.532	8
1941	2	84-70	.545	17
1942	2	93-59	.612	9
1943	7	68-84	.447	29
1944	4	77-77	.500	12
1945	7	71-83	.461	17½
1946	1	104-50	.675	+12
1947	3	83-71	.539	14
1948	2(a)	96-59	.619	1
1949	2	96-58	.623	1
1950	3	94-60	.610	4
1951	3	87-67	.565	11
1952	6	76-78	.494	19
1953	4	84-69	.549	16
1954	4	69-85	.448	42
1955	4	84-70	.545	12
1956	4	84-70	.545	13
1957	3	82-72	.532	16
1958	3	79-75	.513	13
1959	5	75-79	.487	19
1960	7	65-89	.422	32
1961	6	76-86	.469	33
1962	8	76-84	.475	19
1963	7	76-85	.472	28
1964	8	72-90	.444	27
1965	9	62-100	.383	40
1966	9	72-90	.444	26
1967	1	92-70	.568	+ 1
1968	3	86-76	.531	17
1969(b)	3	87-75	.537	22
1970	3	87-75	.537	21
1971	3	85-77	.525	18
1972	2	85-70	.548	½
1973	2	89-73	.549	8
1974	3	84-78	.519	7

(a)—finished regular season tied for first; lost one game playoff to Cleveland.

(b)—first year East Division, American League.

Red Sox Managers

1901-06	James J. Collins
1906	Chick Stahl
1907	Cy Young
	George Huff
	Bob Unglaub
	Deacon McGuire
1908	Deacon McGuire
	Fred Lake
1909	Fred Lake
1910-11	Patsy Donovan
1912	Jake Stahl
1913	Jake Stahl
	Bill Carrigan
1914-16	Bill Carrigan
1917	Jack Barry
1918-20	Edward B. Barrow
1921-22	Hugh Duffy
1923	Frank Chance
1924-26	Leo A. Fohl
1927-29	Bill Carrigan
1930	Heinie Wagner
1931	Shano Collins
1932	Shano Collins
	Marty McManus
1934	Bucky Harris
1935-47	Joe Cronin
1948-49	Joe V. McCarthy
1950	Joe V. McCarthy
	Steve O'Neill
1951	Steve O'Neill
1952-54	Lou Boudreau
1955-58	Mike Higgins
1959	Mike Higgins
	Billy Jurges
1960	Billy Jurges
	Del Baker
	Mike Higgins
1961-62	Mike Higgins
1963	Johnny Pesky
1964	Johnny Pesky
	Billy Herman
1965	Billy Herman
1966	Billy Herman
	Pete Runnels
1967-68	Dick Williams
1969	Dick Williams
	Eddie Popowski
1970-73	Eddie Kasko
1974	Darrell Johnson

Red Sox Career Batting Leaders

Games

T. Williams	2,292
Yastrzemski	2,117

Doerr	1,865	T. Conigliaro	160
Hooper	1,646	R. Smith	149
D. DiMaggio	1,399	Malzone	131
Malzone	1,359	Stephens	122
Petrocelli	1,353		
Lewis	1,184	**RBIs**	
Goodman	1,177	T. Williams	1,839
Cronin	1,134	Doerr	1,247
		Yastrzemski	1,181
At Bats		Foxx	788
Yastrzemski	7,759	Cronin	737
T. Williams	7,706	Jensen	733
Doerr	7,093	Malzone	716
Hooper	6,269	Petrocelli	690
D. DiMaggio	5,640	Lewis	643
Malzone	5,273	D. DiMaggio	618
Petrocelli	4,478		
Goodman	4,399	**Extra Base Hits**	
Lewis	4,325	T. Williams	1,117
Pesky	4,085	Yastrzemski	780
		Doerr	693
Runs		D. DiMaggio	452
T. Williams	1,798	Foxx	448
Yastrzemski	1,240	Petrocelli	435
Doerr	1,094	Cronin	433
D. DiMaggio	1,046	Hooper	406
Hooper	988	Speaker	387
Pesky	776	Malzone	386
Foxx	721	R. Smith	386
Speaker	703		
Goodman	688	**Batting Average**	
Cronin	645	T. Williams	.344
		Speaker	.336
Hits		Foxx	.320
T. Williams	2,654	Runnels	.320
Yastrzemski	2,267	Pesky	.313
Doerr	2,042	Goodman	.306
Hooper	1,707	Cramer	.302
D. DiMaggio	1,680	D. DiMaggio	.298
Malzone	1,454	J. Collins	.296
Goodman	1,344		
Speaker	1,328		
Pesky	1,277		
Lewis	1,248		

Doubles

T. Williams	525	
Yastrzemski	436	
Doerr	381	
D. DiMaggio	308	

Red Sox Career Pitching Leaders

Doubles		Games	
Cronin	270	Kinder	365
Lewis	254	Young	327
Goodman	248	Fornieles	326
Hooper	246	Delock	322
Speaker	241	Parnell*	289
Malzone	234	Radatz	286
		Lyle*	260
Triples		Dobson	259
Hooper	130	J. Wilson	258
Speaker	108	F. Sullivan	252
Freeman	91		
Doerr	89	**Wins**	
Gardner	87	Young	193
Ferris	78	Parnell*	123
T. Williams	71	Wood	112
J. Collins	65	Dobson	106
Parent	63	Grove*	105
Lewis	63	Hughson	96
		Monbouquette	96
Home Runs		Brewer	91
T. Williams	521	F. Sullivan	90
Yastrzemski	303	Collins*	89
Doerr	223	H. Leonard*	89
Foxx	222	Ruth*	89
Petrocelli	200		
Jensen	170		

Losses

Young	112
Winter	97
Ruffing	96
Russell	94
Monbouquette	91
Dineen	85
Brewer	82
F. Sullivan	80
MacFayden	78
Parnell*	75

Innings

Young	2730
Parnell*	1753
Monbouquette	1622
Winter	1598
Dobson	1544
Grove*	1540
Brewer	1510
F. Sullivan	1506
Dineen	1501
Wood	1416

Shutouts

Young	39
Wood	28
H. Leonard*	24
Collins*	20
Parnell*	20
S. Jones	18
Dobson	17
Ruth*	17
Dineen	16
G. Foster	16
Monbouquette	16

Saves

Radatz	103
Kinder	91
Lyle*	63
Fornieles	48
Delock	31
Bolin	28
Kiely*	28
Wyatt	25

Games Started

Young	298
Parnell*	232
Monbouquette	228
F. Sullivan	219
Brewer	217
Dobson	202
Grove*	189
Nixon	177
Dineen	175
Winter	175

Complete Games

Young	276
Dineen	156
Winter	141
Wood	121
Grove*	119
Parnell*	113
Ruth*	105
Hughson	99
H. Leonard*	96
Collins*	90
Dobson	90

Strikeouts

Young	1363

Wood	986
Monbouquette	969
F. Sullivan	821
Culp	794
Lonborg	784
H. Leonard*	769
Grove*	743
Brewer	733
Parnell*	732

Winning Pct. (100 Dec.)

Wood (112-57)	.663
Ruth* (89-46)	.659
Hughson (96-54)	.640
Young (193-112)	.633
Grove* (105-62)	.629
Kinder (86-52)	.623
Parnell* (123-75)	.621
Ferrell (62-40)	.608
Tannehill* (60-40)	.600
Dobson (106-72)	.596

*Left-handers.

Red Sox
20-Game Winners

Cy Young—1901 (31-10), 1902 (32-12), 1903 (28-9), 1904 (26-16), 1907 (22-15), 1908 (21-11)
Bill Dineen—1902 (21-21), 1903 (21-11)
Tom Hughes—1903 (21-7)
Jesse Tannehill—1905 (22-9)
Joe Wood—1911 (23-17), 1912 (34-5)
Hugh Bedient—1912 (20-12)
Ray Collins—1914 (20-13)
George Foster—1915 (20-9)
Babe Ruth—1916 (23-12), 1917 (23-17)
Carl Mays—1917 (22-9), 1918 (21-13)
Sam Jones—1921 (23-16)
Howard Ehmke—1923 (20-17)
Lefty Grove—1935 (20-12)
Wes Ferrell—1935 (25-14), 1936 (20-15)
Tex Hughson—1942 (22-6), 1946 (20-11)
Boo Ferriss—1945 (22-10), 1946 (25-6)
Mel Parnell—1949 (25-7), 1953 (21-8)
Ellis Kinder—1949 (23-6)
Bill Monbouquette—1963 (20-10)
Jim Lonborg—1967 (22-9)
Luis Tiant—1973 (20-13)

Red Sox
League Leaders

Batting Champions
Dale Alexander—1932
  (including 32 games with Detroit)
Jimmie Foxx—1938
Ted Williams—1941-42, 1947-48, 1957-58
Billy Goodman—1950
Pete Runnels—1960, 1962
Carl Yastrzemski—1963, 1967-68

Home Run Champions
Buck Freeman—1903
Jake Stahl—1910
Babe Ruth—1918 (tie), 1919
Jimmie Foxx—1939
Ted Williams—1941-42, 1947, 1949
Tony Conigliaro—1965
Carl Yastrzemski—1967 (tie)

RBI Champions
Babe Ruth—1919
Jimmie Foxx—1938
Ted Williams—1939, 1942, 1947, 1949
  (tie)
Vern Stephens—1949 (tie), 1950 (tie)
Walt Dropo—1950 (tie)
Jackie Jensen—1955 (tie), 1958-59
Dick Stuart—1963
Carl Yastrzemski—1967
Ken Harrelson—1968

Red Sox
World Series Record

1903—Red Sox beat Pittsburgh
  Pirates 5-3.
1912—Red Sox beat New York Giants
  4-3 (1 tie).
1915—Red Sox beat Philadelphia
  Athletics 4-1.
1916—Red Sox beat Brooklyn
  Dodgers 4-1.
1918—Red Sox beat Chicago Cubs
  4-2.
1946—St. Louis Cardinals beat
  Red Sox 4-3.
1967—St. Louis Cardinals beat
  Red Sox 4-3.

Acknowledgments
My thanks to Bill Crowley and the rest of the Red Sox' public relations department for their assistance and encouragement.

Photo Credits

Walter Jooss, Jr., Sports Illustrated © **Time, Inc.** front cover
Boston Public Library 1, 42-44, 44-45 center, 46, 46-47 bottom, 50-51, 55
Boston Red Sox 15 right, 20 top, 21, 45 right, 47 top, 54 bottom, 61 bottom, 75, 87 top, 98, 105 center and right, 106-7, 110, 113 right, 126, 144, 146 top, 158, 160, 168 insert, 179, back cover top
United Press International 2-5, 10-11, 14-15 center, 16-18, 20 bottom, 23, 25-31, 33-39, 48, 53, 54 top, 57, 59, 61 top left and right, 62-63, 65-68, 70-71, 73, 76, 79, 81, 85, 87 bottom, 88-89, 91, 93-95, 101, 103, 105 left, 111, 113 left, 115, 118-19, 124, 127-29, 131, 135-36, 140-41, 143, 146 bottom, 148-49, 151, 153, 155, 157, 159, 161-65, 167, 168 main photo, 172-73, 177, 180, back cover middle and bottom